Golden State Blues

A Comprehensive Guide to

Gavin Newsom's Political Record

Ahead of His 2028 Campaign

Connor Strickland

In today's fast-paced world, the flow of information is relentless. News comes down the pike at a speed few can process, creating an overwhelming barrage of headlines, opinions, and hot takes. As the media landscape grows more fragmented, the challenge of discerning truth from spin, objectivity from bias, becomes increasingly daunting.

This book aims to cut through the noise. As a conservative, I approach this subject from a particular viewpoint, but my goal is to present the facts as objectively as possible. This is not about promoting an agenda—it's about providing readers with the information they need to make informed decisions about one of the most pivotal figures in American politics today: California Governor Gavin Newsom.

We're coming off a presidential election in which Democratic voters didn't even get a say in their party's candidate. Vice President Kamala Harris argued that her loss was due to a lack of time to run a proper campaign. Yet, the numbers suggest something more troubling: the longer voters had to evaluate her leadership, the less they seemed to support her.

Now, all eyes are on 2028. Gavin Newsom stands as one of the most likely contenders for the Democratic nomination, rivaled only by Kamala Harris herself. Unlike Harris's truncated campaign, Newsom has the advantage of time—a full four years for voters to get to know him, to understand his record, and to consider his vision for the country.

This book offers a head start. It is an opportunity for voters to look beyond the headlines and the soundbites, to examine Gavin Newsom's California today, and to contemplate what it might mean for America tomorrow. Whether you agree with his policies or not, the stakes are too high to walk into the next presidential election uninformed.

Let's begin.

Roadmap for the Reader

This book provides a detailed, in-depth examination of Gavin Newsom's political career and the policies he has implemented during his time as Governor of California, assessing how his leadership may shape the future of the nation should he be elected as president. As one of the most prominent figures in American politics today, Newsom's actions in California have drawn national attention, making it crucial to understand the full scope of his record before the 2028 presidential race.

Here's what you can expect:

Chapter 1: The Age of Information Overload

We begin by examining the modern media landscape and the challenges it presents in discerning fact from spin. This chapter sets the stage for the book, emphasizing the need to critically evaluate political figures and their policies in the age of rapid information flow. It also explains the motivation for this book, urging readers to go beyond surface-level perceptions and dive deeper into Newsom's record to understand the potential implications of his future political ambitions.

Chapter 2: Early Life and Political Ascent

In this chapter, we explore Gavin Newsom's background, from his childhood and early struggles to his rise in California politics. We look at the pivotal moments that shaped his worldview, leadership style, and political trajectory. From his time as a San Francisco supervisor to his role as mayor and Lieutenant Governor, we trace how Newsom navigated California's political landscape and built the foundation for his progressive vision.

Chapter 3: Governorship of California 2019-Present

This is the heart of the book: a critical evaluation of Newsom's leadership as Governor of California. We explore the major initiatives he has implemented in areas like climate change, healthcare, homelessness, and criminal justice. We also examine the controversies and challenges that have defined his time in office, assessing how his policies have impacted the state and the lives of its residents. This chapter provides insight into the effectiveness of Newsom's governance and offers lessons for his potential role on the national stage.

Chapter 4: Progressive Stance on Transgenderism

This chapter takes an in-depth look at Gavin Newsom's stance on transgender issues, including his support for transgender rights, policies surrounding transgender youth, participation in sports, and access to what calls healthcare. We explore the implications of these policies, particularly the controversial aspects, and critically evaluate how Newsom's approach to transgenderism may affect both California and the nation. This chapter aims to provide a nuanced understanding of the challenges and debates surrounding these policies.

Chapter 5: The Future of California

In this chapter, we analyze California's future under Newsom's leadership. We examine the long-term effects of his policies on the state's economy, social fabric, and governance. This section also reflects on the lessons to be drawn from California's experience under Newsom and whether his policies could be replicated or scaled to a national level. It provides a lens through which to assess Newsom's broader vision for America and his readiness to lead on the national stage.

Chapter 6: The 2028 Question

The short & final chapter addresses Gavin Newsom's potential candidacy for president in 2028. We assess his political strengths and vulnerabilities, exploring the challenges he may face as he seeks to transition from California governor to national leader. This chapter evaluates Newsom's ability to unite a divided nation, his appeal to a broader electorate, and the lessons voters can draw from his leadership in California. We conclude by reflecting on Newsom's readiness for the presidency and what his candidacy could mean for the future of the United States.

Throughout this book, the goal is not to persuade you to support or oppose Gavin Newsom but to provide a detailed, fact-based assessment of his leadership and policies. Whether you agree with his progressive vision or have reservations about his approach, this book invites you to critically evaluate the potential impact of a leader who may one day shape the future of the United States.

Chapter 1

The Age of Information Overload

In the digital age, information moves faster than ever. News cycles churn at breakneck speed, flooding our devices with updates, opinions, and breaking headlines. Social media amplifies this noise, blending fact with speculation until it's nearly impossible to distinguish one from the other. Competing outlets vie for our attention, each claiming authority, each shaping narratives to fit their audience's preferences. Amid this chaos, the challenge of discerning truth from spin, and objective reporting from partisan bias, has grown immensely.

This overwhelming flow of information creates a dangerous paradox: while we're more connected than at any point in history, we're also more susceptible to misinformation and fatigue. The result? Critical issues get buried beneath sensationalist headlines, and voters often feel ill-equipped to make informed decisions.

The stakes are especially high when it comes to choosing our leaders. Governors, senators, and presidents shape the trajectory of our nation, and yet, too often, their campaigns are defined by soundbites rather than substance. In the most recent presidential election, many Democratic voters felt they had no real say in selecting their candidate. Kamala Harris, thrust into the race at the eleventh hour, lamented that she lacked sufficient time to connect with voters. Yet, the truth may be simpler—and more telling: the more time people had to evaluate her, the less convinced they became.

Looking ahead to 2028, Gavin Newsom stands as one of the Democratic Party's most likely contenders for the presidency. He is charismatic, well-spoken, and a masterful campaigner. But these qualities, while undeniably important, are not enough. What matters most is how he has governed, how his policies have shaped California, and what his leadership says about the kind of president he would be.

This book is an opportunity to take a step back from the noise. It's a chance to critically examine Gavin Newsom's record, to explore the successes and failures of his time in office, and to consider what his California means for America's future. The goal is simple: to provide voters with an informed, objective lens through which to view a potential president—not the polished campaign image, but the leader behind it.

In a world drowning in information, clarity is a rare and precious thing. This book is my effort to provide it.

Purpose of the Book

The goal of this book is not to attack Gavin Newsom personally. It is not to tear down his character or diminish the undeniable talents that have propelled him to the national stage. Newsom is, by any measure, a compelling political figure. He is charismatic, articulate, and adept at connecting with audiences. These qualities have made him a formidable presence in American politics and a likely contender for the Democratic nomination in 2028.

But as voters, it is our responsibility to look beyond surface-level appeal. A winning smile and a polished speech can sway hearts, but they are not measures of effective leadership. Leadership is defined by the decisions made in moments of crisis, the policies enacted to solve real-world problems, and the ability to balance ambition with accountability. It is in these areas that we must evaluate Gavin Newsom—not as the polished candidate he may present himself to be, but as the governor he has been.

California, under Newsom's leadership, offers a unique lens through which to assess his potential as a national leader. As one of the largest economies in the world and a microcosm of America's diversity, California is both a beacon of opportunity and a site of significant challenges. From climate change to housing affordability, homelessness to public safety, the state has grappled with some of the most pressing issues of our time. Newsom's tenure as governor has shaped the trajectory of these challenges, for better or worse, and provides valuable insights into his vision, priorities, and ability to deliver results.

This book is an opportunity to critically examine that record. It is not about partisan ideology but about performance—about how Newsom has governed and what his California might tell us about a future under his leadership as president. By looking beyond the charisma, the eloquence, and the media-savvy image, we can uncover the substance of his policies and governance.

Ultimately, this book is for voters. It is for those who believe that leadership should be earned through a proven ability to address complex problems, not through optics and persuasion alone. Gavin Newsom is an undeniably strong candidate, but before he becomes a national leader, we owe it to ourselves—and our country—to understand the full picture. This is our chance to do just that.

Early Life: A Blend of Privilege and Challenges

Gavin Newsom's story begins in San Francisco, a city that would later serve as the launchpad for his political career. Born on October 10, 1967, into a family with deep ties to the city's political and social elite, Newsom's early years were marked by both privilege and adversity. His father, William Newsom, was a state appeals court judge and a close friend of the Getty family—one of America's wealthiest dynasties. This connection would later open doors for Gavin, including business ventures funded by the Gettys. However, despite these advantages, his childhood was far from seamless.

When Gavin was ten years old, his parents divorced. The split profoundly impacted his family, leaving his mother, Tessa Newsom, to raise him and his younger sister, Hilary, largely on her own. Tessa worked multiple jobs to support the family, instilling in Gavin a deep respect for resilience and hard work. Watching his mother juggle the challenges of single parenthood while maintaining her unwavering dedication to her children became a defining influence in his life.

Struggles with Dyslexia: A Test of Perseverance

Academically, Gavin faced significant challenges due to severe dyslexia, a condition that would shape his outlook and work ethic for years to come. Words often appeared jumbled, and reading—a cornerstone of academic success—became an uphill battle. The condition made school difficult and, at times, deeply frustrating. He struggled with traditional learning methods, often feeling out of step with his peers. Teachers would later recall his determination to overcome these obstacles, even if it meant spending hours deciphering what others could read in minutes.

Rather than succumbing to his challenges, Newsom developed a relentless drive to succeed. Dyslexia forced him to think differently, to adapt, and to approach problems with creativity and resilience—traits that would serve him well in both business and politics. To this day, he credits his struggles with dyslexia for instilling in him a strong sense of discipline and the ability to persevere under pressure.

Shaped by His Environment

Growing up in San Francisco during the 1970s and 80s, Gavin was exposed to the city's cultural and political vibrancy. He witnessed its economic disparities and social movements firsthand, experiences that would later inform his progressive political vision. Despite his family's connections, Newsom worked hard to carve out his own identity. He took on various jobs as a teenager, including selling shoes and working at a local restaurant, experiences that gave him a taste of the working-class realities often hidden from those in privileged circles.

Newsom's early life is a study in contrasts: privilege tempered by struggle, and advantage counterbalanced by personal adversity. These formative experiences helped shape the man who would later rise to lead California, combining an acute awareness of inequality with the discipline to tackle it head-on. As we examine his leadership in the chapters ahead, it's important to understand the forces that forged his character and the values he carries with him into public service.

California: A Microcosm of America's Future

California, often referred to as the "Golden State," holds a unique position in the American imagination. With its vast size, diverse population, and economic clout, California is more than just one of fifty states—it's often seen as a glimpse into America's future. The state's policies, innovations, and challenges tend to ripple across the nation, shaping cultural, economic, and political trends. Under Governor Gavin Newsom's leadership, California has cemented its role as both a testing ground for progressive ideals and a cautionary tale for the complexities of governing in a polarized age.

The Progressive Experiment

California has long been a laboratory for ambitious policies aimed at addressing some of the nation's most pressing issues. From pioneering climate change initiatives to enacting sweeping social justice reforms, the state has positioned itself as a leader in progressive governance. Newsom, as governor, has embraced this role wholeheartedly. His administration has pushed forward landmark legislation on issues ranging from renewable energy to healthcare access, often positioning California as a counterweight to more conservative states and federal policies.

For many, California represents what America could become: a place where diversity is celebrated, where innovation thrives, and where the government is unafraid to take bold action. Newsom's tenure has been marked by an emphasis on tackling inequality, protecting marginalized communities, and leading the charge on environmental sustainability. These are the credentials he will likely present to voters as a presidential candidate—a vision of progress and possibility.

A Cautionary Tale

But California is also a state of contradictions. Despite its wealth and innovation, it faces some of the most intractable challenges in the nation. Housing affordability has reached crisis levels, with millions of residents struggling to find or maintain stable housing. Homelessness continues to rise, starkly visible on the streets of its major cities. Public safety concerns and economic inequality further complicate the picture. These issues, while not unique to California, are amplified by the state's size and influence, making them a litmus test for the effectiveness of its leadership.

Newsom's record as governor is inseparable from these challenges. While his supporters point to his ambitious agenda, critics argue that the results often fall short of the promises. For every groundbreaking climate initiative, there are accusations of bureaucratic inefficiency or mismanagement. For every social justice victory, there are questions about sustainability and unintended consequences. California's experiment in progressive governance offers both inspiration and warnings—lessons that are crucial for understanding Newsom's potential as a national leader.

Setting the Stage

As Gavin Newsom looks to the national stage, his tenure in California provides a preview of the kind of president he might be. Will he bring the innovative spirit of California's successes to the White House? Or will he be weighed down by the unresolved issues that have plagued his governorship? These are the questions this book seeks to answer.

California's story is, in many ways, America's story: a nation grappling with change, striving for progress, and wrestling with its contradictions. In examining Newsom's leadership, we gain not only insights into his potential presidency but also a deeper understanding of the broader challenges facing the country. If California is a microcosm of America's future, then Newsom's record is a roadmap—one we cannot afford to ignore.

Why This Book Matters

As the nation looks toward the 2028 presidential election, the stakes could not be higher. Gavin Newsom has emerged as one of the Democratic Party's most compelling figures and a likely front-runner for the nomination. With his charisma, eloquence, and commanding presence, he is well-positioned to capture the imagination of voters across the political spectrum. His speeches are polished, his campaign appearances carefully orchestrated, and his image meticulously crafted. In many ways, he is the quintessential modern candidate—handsome, persuasive, and media-savvy.

But elections should be about more than appearances and soundbites. While Newsom's strengths as a communicator are undeniable, voters must look beyond the surface to understand the substance of his leadership. What does his record tell us about his ability to deliver on promises? How have his policies impacted the millions of people he governs in California? And perhaps most importantly, how would his leadership translate to the national stage?

The stakes are especially high because of the lessons learned from recent elections. Vice President Kamala Harris, a fellow Californian, faced significant challenges during her campaign, with many voters expressing regret over not having enough time to assess her candidacy. The reality, however, was more nuanced: the more time voters had to evaluate Harris, the less confident they became in her leadership. This underscores the importance of giving voters the information they need—not at the eleventh hour, but years in advance—to make informed decisions about who will lead the nation.

This book aims to provide that head start. It is an opportunity to examine Gavin Newsom's record as governor, to weigh his accomplishments against his challenges, and to critically assess the vision he brings to the table. His leadership of California offers valuable insights into how he might govern as president—insights that voters deserve to have before they step into the voting booth.

Gavin Newsom is a formidable candidate. His charisma, combined with his ability to articulate a compelling vision, makes him a serious contender. But charisma alone is not enough. As voters, we have a responsibility to dig deeper, to ask tough questions, and to consider the broader implications of his policies and leadership style. This book is a guide for that process, an invitation to look beyond the campaign trail and into the heart of what truly matters: leadership that is not only inspiring but also effective.

In an age of political theater, the future of the nation depends on our ability to see through the show and focus on the substance. Gavin Newsom's candidacy deserves a thorough examination, and this book is here to ensure that happens.

Chapter 2

Early Life and Political Ascent

Gavin Newsom was born into a family deeply embedded in San Francisco's cultural and political fabric. His father, William Newsom, was a state appeals court judge and a longtime confidant of the Getty family, one of America's most prominent and affluent dynasties. These connections would later open significant doors for Newsom, providing opportunities that shaped his trajectory in business and politics. However, Newsom's upbringing wasn't solely defined by privilege—it was also marked by personal challenges that influenced his character and work ethic.

In 1977, when Gavin was just ten years old, his parents divorced—a turning point in his young life. Following the separation, his mother, Tessa Newsom, became the bedrock of the family. Working multiple jobs to make ends meet, Tessa embodied resilience and determination, qualities that left a lasting impression on her son. Gavin often credits his mother's unwavering work ethic with instilling in him a deep appreciation for perseverance and the value of hard work, lessons he carried into adulthood.

Despite the hardships at home, the family's connection to the Gettys provided unique opportunities. The Getty family not only supported Gavin's father professionally but also helped fund Gavin's early entrepreneurial ventures, including the launch of the PlumpJack wine business. This venture marked Gavin's first major step into the public eye, blending his business acumen with his ability to build influential networks. While these connections have sometimes drawn criticism for giving him a privileged start, they also highlight his ability to capitalize on opportunities and navigate high-stakes environments.

Growing up in San Francisco during a time of social and political upheaval, Gavin was exposed to both the city's vibrant culture and its glaring inequalities. This dichotomy of privilege and struggle would shape his worldview and influence the policies he championed later in his career. From his mother's determination to the Gettys' support, his upbringing forged a complex foundation—one that blends resilience, ambition, and a keen understanding of the power of networks.

Education and Early Career

After completing high school, Gavin Newsom attended Santa Clara University, a Jesuit institution known for its commitment to ethics and social justice. While pursuing a degree in political science, Newsom was drawn to questions about governance, public service, and the intersection of policy and business. His time at Santa Clara deepened his interest in leadership and sharpened his understanding of the challenges facing communities like his own in San Francisco.

It wasn't just academics that shaped Newsom during these years. Santa Clara's Jesuit values—emphasizing service to others and moral responsibility—aligned with his growing ambition to make a meaningful impact. These principles would later influence his approach to policy making, particularly in areas like housing and social equity.

After graduating in 1989, Newsom's first steps into the professional world were marked by a desire to create something of his own. He co-founded the PlumpJack Group, starting with a small wine shop in San Francisco. While the venture grew into a successful chain of wineries, hotels, and restaurants, it also gave

Newsom a crash course in leadership, risk-taking, and the realities of managing complex operations. These early experiences taught him how to navigate challenges, build coalitions, and turn ambitious ideas into practical outcomes—skills he would carry into his political career.

Beyond the business's success, PlumpJack became a platform for Newsom to connect with the city's influential figures. It wasn't just about making money; it was about building relationships and establishing a public profile. Through these efforts, he began to bridge the gap between private enterprise and public service, setting the stage for his eventual leap into politics.

Political Beginnings: San Francisco Supervisor

Gavin Newsom's entry into politics began in 1996, when then-Mayor Willie Brown appointed him to the San Francisco Parking and Traffic Commission. Though seemingly a low-profile position, this appointment marked Newsom's first step into public service and provided him with an opportunity to prove his commitment to the city. He quickly distinguished himself as a proactive and engaged commissioner, impressing Mayor Brown with his ability to navigate bureaucracy and find pragmatic solutions to local issues.

A year later, Newsom was appointed to fill a vacant seat on the San Francisco Board of Supervisors, the legislative body responsible for governing the city and county of San Francisco. At 29 years old, he became one of the youngest people to serve in this role. His appointment was strategic—Brown recognized Newsom's combination of business savvy, charisma, and connections as an asset to the city's leadership.

Running for Election and Solidifying His Position

Newsom officially ran for the seat in 1998 and won, earning the support of both business leaders and a growing base of local voters. His campaign emphasized practical governance, blending his business background with a progressive vision for the city. Newsom's ability to appeal to both the city's elite and its working-class voters demonstrated his early skill as a unifying figure, capable of bridging diverse constituencies.

As a supervisor, Newsom represented District 2, which included some of San Francisco's wealthiest neighborhoods. While his district leaned affluent, Newsom didn't limit his focus to issues affecting only the privileged. Instead, he began crafting a political identity that balanced progressive ideals with a pragmatic, results-oriented approach.

Key Policies and Initiatives

During his time on the Board of Supervisors, Newsom introduced several key policies that reflected his emerging vision for governance. Among his most notable efforts was the Care Not Cash initiative, aimed at addressing San Francisco's growing homelessness crisis. The initiative proposed redirecting cash payments given to homeless individuals into funding for shelter, housing, and supportive services. Newsom argued that the existing system was failing both the city and its homeless population, as cash payments often failed to address the root causes of homelessness.

While Care Not Cash became a cornerstone of Newsom's tenure as a supervisor, it was also highly controversial. Critics accused the policy of being overly punitive and failing to consider the broader systemic issues driving homelessness. Supporters, however, praised it as a bold attempt to reform a broken system and to shift resources toward more sustainable solutions. The initiative underscored Newsom's willingness to take on politically sensitive issues and to stand by his proposals, even in the face of significant opposition.

In addition to his work on homelessness, Newsom championed policies aimed at improving public health and safety. He supported early efforts to expand access to healthcare services for underserved communities and advocated for programs to reduce gun violence in the city. These initiatives highlighted his commitment to addressing social inequality while maintaining a pragmatic focus on actionable solutions.

Shaping His Progressive Identity

Newsom's time as a supervisor laid the foundation for his progressive political identity. He positioned himself as a problem-solver who could tackle the city's most pressing challenges with creativity and determination. His blend of progressive values and business acumen set him apart from his peers, earning him both allies and critics within San Francisco's political establishment.

Throughout his tenure, Newsom demonstrated an ability to navigate the complexities of local government while building relationships with key stakeholders. His work on the Board of Supervisors not only solidified his reputation as a rising political star but also prepared him for the larger stage he would soon step onto as San Francisco's mayor.

The Willie Brown Connection

Willie Brown's influence in California politics cannot be overstated. A towering figure in the Democratic Party, Brown served as Speaker of the California State Assembly for 15 years before becoming Mayor of San Francisco in 1996. His charisma, political acumen, and ability to build alliances made him a kingmaker in California politics. Among those who benefitted from his mentorship and connections were Gavin Newsom and Kamala Harris, two figures whose political paths intertwined with Brown's during pivotal moments in their careers.

Gavin Newsom's Mentor

For Gavin Newsom, Willie Brown was a key figure in his early political ascent. In 1996, Brown appointed Newsom to the San Francisco Parking and Traffic Commission, giving him his first taste of public service. Just a year later, Brown elevated Newsom again, appointing him to the San Francisco Board of Supervisors to fill a vacant seat. These moves not only positioned Newsom as a rising star in San Francisco politics but also introduced him to the inner workings of city governance.

Brown's support was instrumental in launching Newsom's career. His appointments gave Newsom credibility, visibility, and the opportunity to build a political base. While Newsom's connections to the Getty family provided financial backing and networking opportunities, Brown's endorsement offered a stamp of approval from one of California's most powerful Democrats.

Kamala Harris's Rise

Around the same time, Brown's relationship with Kamala Harris was also shaping her early career. Harris, then a young prosecutor, was romantically involved with Brown during the mid-1990s while he was Speaker of the Assembly and married to Blanche Vitero, his wife of over 30 years. Though separated, Brown and his wife remained legally married throughout his relationship with Harris. This extramarital affair drew public scrutiny, particularly as Brown used his political influence to advance Harris's career.

During their relationship, Brown appointed Harris to two state boards: the California Unemployment Insurance Appeals Board and the Medical Assistance Commission. These positions provided her with valuable experience and increased her profile, though critics argued that her appointments were a result of favoritism rather than merit. Harris later downplayed the relationship, attempting to emphasize her own qualifications and hard work as the foundation of her success.

The Intersection of Influence

The connections between Willie Brown, Gavin Newsom, and Kamala Harris highlight the intertwined nature of California politics. Brown's role as a mentor, benefactor, and, at times, controversial figure underscores the complicated dynamics of power and influence. While both Newsom and Harris eventually emerged as independent political leaders, their early ties to Brown remain a significant part of their stories.

For Newsom, Brown's appointments laid the groundwork for his political career, allowing him to establish himself as a pragmatic, business-oriented progressive. For Harris, the relationship brought both opportunities and criticism, shaping the narrative around her rise in public life.

Legacy and Controversy

Willie Brown's infidelity and willingness to wield his influence for protégés like Newsom and Harris reflect both the opportunities and the pitfalls of political patronage. His actions contributed to the successes of two major Democratic figures, but they also raised questions about the ethics of such relationships. For voters evaluating the leadership of Gavin Newsom or Kamala Harris, understanding their early connections to Brown offers insight into the networks and alliances that shaped their paths to power.

San Francisco Mayor: Bold Moves and Controversy

In 2004, Gavin Newsom became the youngest Mayor of San Francisco in a century. At just 36 years old, his rise to the city's highest office marked him as a bold and ambitious leader eager to make a mark on both the city and the national stage. His tenure as mayor would be defined by groundbreaking decisions, sweeping reforms, and the inevitable controversies that accompany high-profile leadership.

Legalizing Same-Sex Marriage: A Defining Moment

Newsom's most defining moment as mayor came early in his tenure. In February 2004, just a month after taking office, he directed the San Francisco City Clerk's office to issue marriage licenses to same-sex couples, defying state law at the time. This decision made San Francisco the first city in the United States to officially recognize same-sex marriages, positioning Newsom as a progressive icon and a champion of LGBTQ+ rights.

The move was as daring as it was controversial. Over the course of the next month, more than 4,000 same-sex couples flocked to City Hall to exchange vows, creating an unprecedented wave of marriages that captured national and international attention. Newsom's action drew praise from progressives and LGBTQ+ activists, who celebrated his willingness to challenge entrenched legal and societal norms. For many, it was a watershed moment in the fight for marriage equality, one that set the stage for broader legal battles and eventual victories, including the U.S. Supreme Court's 2015 decision to legalize same-sex marriage nationwide.

However, Newsom's decision also sparked backlash. Conservative groups, religious organizations, and political opponents criticized his move as an overreach of executive authority. Lawsuits were filed, and the California Supreme Court eventually invalidated the marriages, ruling that Newsom had exceeded his legal powers. Despite this setback, Newsom's boldness cemented his reputation as a leader unafraid to take risks for his convictions, even at great personal and political cost.

Governing in a Divided City

While Newsom's stance on same-sex marriage earned him national acclaim, his time as mayor was not without significant challenges. San Francisco, a city known for its progressive ideals, also grappled with deep-rooted issues that tested Newsom's ability to balance ambition with practical governance.

One of the most contentious issues during his tenure was homelessness. Newsom championed his Care Not Cash initiative, which redirected cash welfare payments for homeless individuals into services like housing and healthcare. While the policy aimed to address the root causes of homelessness, it drew sharp criticism from advocacy groups who argued that it criminalized poverty and failed to adequately address systemic inequalities. Supporters, however, lauded the program as a necessary reform in a city struggling with visible and persistent homelessness.

In addition to homelessness, Newsom faced scrutiny over his administration's handling of housing affordability and public safety. San Francisco's soaring property values and increasing economic inequality posed significant challenges, leading to debates over gentrification and the displacement of long-time residents. Critics accused Newsom of prioritizing the interests of developers and business elites, while supporters pointed to his efforts to expand affordable housing and streamline permitting processes as evidence of his commitment to addressing the crisis.

Balancing Ambition and Leadership

Newsom's tenure as mayor revealed both the strengths and vulnerabilities of his leadership style. His willingness to take bold, high-profile stands—such as his push for same-sex marriage—demonstrated his ability to galvanize support and drive progressive change. However, his focus on ambitious initiatives sometimes drew attention away from the day-to-day challenges of governance, leaving him open to criticism from those who felt his priorities were misaligned with the city's most pressing needs.

Despite these controversies, Newsom's time as mayor served as a springboard for his political career. It solidified his reputation as a trailblazer on social issues, while also highlighting the complexities of governing in a city as diverse and divided as San Francisco. For better or worse, his tenure offered a glimpse of the boldness and ambition he would bring to higher office—a style of leadership that continues to define him today.

Positioning for Statewide Office

Gavin Newsom's tenure as San Francisco's mayor not only shaped his leadership style but also served as a launchpad for his ambitions beyond the city. Throughout his two terms, Newsom demonstrated a keen ability to build alliances, leverage his progressive credentials, and position himself as a rising star in California politics. By the time he announced his candidacy for Lieutenant Governor in 2009, he had established himself as a politician with statewide appeal.

Building Alliances and Expanding His Base

As mayor, Newsom cultivated relationships with influential figures across California's political and business landscapes. His early connection to former Mayor Willie Brown remained a valuable asset, giving him access to key Democratic networks. Simultaneously, his business background and connections to the Getty family helped solidify his standing among the state's financial elite.

Newsom's progressive policy agenda, particularly his advocacy for marriage equality, also earned him national recognition. By taking bold stances on issues like LGBTQ+ rights and homelessness reform, he became a favorite among progressive voters and activists. His ability to connect with both grassroots movements and corporate stakeholders demonstrated a versatility that set him apart from other local leaders.

Beyond policy, Newsom proved to be a master of public relations. His polished image, media savvy, and ability to articulate a clear vision allowed him to transcend the role of mayor and position himself as a leader capable of addressing issues on a larger stage. He often framed San Francisco as a microcosm of California, using his city's successes and challenges as a narrative for what he could achieve statewide.

A Calculated Run for Lieutenant Governor

By the end of his mayoral tenure, Newsom's ambitions for higher office were clear. In 2009, he initially announced his candidacy for Governor of California, seeking to replace outgoing Governor Arnold Schwarzenegger. However, facing stiff competition from former Governor Jerry Brown, Newsom recalibrated his strategy and instead ran for Lieutenant Governor—a position that would allow him to maintain a statewide profile while avoiding a direct confrontation with Brown, who was a heavy favorite in the gubernatorial race.

Newsom's campaign for Lieutenant Governor emphasized his accomplishments as mayor, particularly his progressive initiatives and ability to drive change. While the role of Lieutenant Governor is often seen as largely ceremonial, Newsom framed it as a platform for innovation and advocacy. His campaign promised to bring a fresh perspective to the position, leveraging it to address critical issues such as economic inequality, education reform, and environmental sustainability.

Strategic Moves as Lieutenant Governor

Elected in 2010, Newsom used his time as Lieutenant Governor to further his statewide reach and prepare for a future gubernatorial bid. Though the position lacked executive authority, Newsom found ways to stay in the spotlight. He served as an outspoken advocate on issues like clean energy, job creation, and education reform, frequently clashing with the Republican-controlled federal government during the early years of his tenure.

Newsom also focused on maintaining visibility through media appearances and public events, carefully crafting an image of a proactive leader ready to take on greater responsibilities. His ability to navigate the constraints of the office while building a progressive policy platform underscored his strategic acumen.

Setting the Stage for Governorship

By the time Newsom announced his candidacy for Governor in 2015, he had spent nearly two decades building a political brand that resonated with California voters. His combination of progressive values, business experience, and media-savvy leadership made him a formidable candidate. Leveraging his accomplishments as mayor and Lieutenant Governor, Newsom positioned himself as a forward-thinking leader capable of addressing the state's most pressing challenges.

Newsom's path to the governorship was not without obstacles, but his ability to build alliances, expand his base, and maintain a high profile ensured his success. His time as mayor and Lieutenant Governor had prepared him for the complexities of leading California, while also solidifying his reputation as one of the Democratic Party's most prominent figures.

Gavin Newsom's journey from San Francisco Supervisor to Mayor and eventually Lieutenant Governor showcases a leader who understood the value of bold ideas, strategic alliances, and calculated ambition. These early roles not only shaped his political identity but also laid the groundwork for his rise to governorship. With each step, Newsom honed his ability to navigate complex issues, connect with diverse constituencies, and position himself as a progressive voice for California and beyond. His ascent was not without controversy, but it underscored a clear trajectory: a leader preparing for the national stage.

Chapter 3

Governorship of California (2019–Present)

Gavin Newsom has made combating what he calls a "climate crisis" a cornerstone of his governorship. His administration set some of the most ambitious environmental targets in the nation, including a mandate to achieve carbon neutrality by 2045 and a ban on the sale of new gasoline-powered vehicles by 2035. While touted as forward-thinking by Newsom and his supporters, these policies have drawn sharp criticism for their economic implications and feasibility.

The ban on gas vehicles, in particular, has sparked intense debate. Critics argue that such a policy would impose significant financial burdens on both consumers and businesses. The upfront cost of electric vehicles (EVs) remains substantially higher than that of traditional gas-powered cars, making them inaccessible for many middle- and lower-income Californians. Additionally, the infrastructure required to support a widespread transition to EVs—such as charging stations and grid upgrades—remains underdeveloped, raising concerns about the practicality of implementing the policy statewide.

Recently, Newsom's policies have also been criticized for their selective approach to supporting electric vehicles. In a notable example, Tesla, the only major electric vehicle manufacturer in California, was excluded from his proposed EV tax credit bill. This move has sparked accusations of personal animosity toward Elon Musk, Tesla's CEO, rather than a commitment to supporting California-based businesses. Despite Tesla's crucial role in California's push for electric vehicle adoption, Newsom's exclusion of the company from the bill has raised eyebrows. Critics argue that this decision was driven less by policy and more by Musk's increasingly vocal political stances and departure from California for Texas. By excluding Tesla, Newsom's administration has inadvertently undermined its own goal of advancing the state's electric vehicle industry and further deepened the divide between the state's leadership and its most prominent innovator in green technology.

Economic experts have also raised alarms about the ripple effects of his ban on industries tied to gasoline vehicles. From auto repair shops to fuel distribution networks, many businesses could face closures or job losses as the state shifts away from gas-powered transportation. Critics point to the hypocrisy of enforcing such mandates while California's electric grid struggles to meet existing demand, with rolling blackouts becoming a recurring issue during peak energy usage periods.

Even Newsom himself has acknowledged these challenges, stating, "Transitioning away from gas vehicles is no small task, but it's essential if we want to tackle climate change." However, opponents argue that the move prioritizes ideological goals over economic stability, particularly in a state already grappling with high costs of living and significant income inequality.

Wildfire Prevention: Efforts and Criticisms

California's wildfire crisis has been a persistent issue for decades, exacerbated by population growth in fire-prone areas and long-term forest mismanagement. While Newsom often links the state's worsening wildfires to climate change, many experts point to more immediate causes, including the accumulation of fuel from years of inadequate forest thinning and prescribed burns. These preventable conditions have allowed minor ignitions to escalate into massive, destructive fires.

During his tenure, Newsom has dedicated substantial resources to wildfire prevention, allocating $2 billion in the 2021 and 2022 budgets for forest management and firefighting capabilities. He also expanded prescribed burning programs, a proven method of reducing wildfire fuel. However, his administration faced backlash when an investigation revealed that California had completed only 13% of the wildfire prevention projects it had reported—a stark reminder of the gap between rhetoric and results.

Newsom's wildfire strategy has not been without political controversy. In a notable bipartisan moment, he thanked then-President Donald Trump for providing federal support during the devastating 2020 wildfire season. "I want to acknowledge the work you've done to be proactive in your support," Newsom told Trump during a meeting. While some praised this collaboration, others saw it as an admission of California's reliance on federal resources despite its significant state budget.

Critics also argue that Newsom's focus on long-term climate policies, such as renewable energy goals, often overshadows the immediate need for more effective wildfire mitigation. The state's failure to adequately address basic forest management practices, such as clearing underbrush and maintaining firebreaks, has left many Californians vulnerable to increasingly severe fire seasons. While Newsom frames wildfires as part of the broader climate crisis, skeptics maintain that his administration's mismanagement has been a more significant factor in the state's inability to reduce the frequency and scale of these disasters.

Healthcare Reforms and COVID-19 Response

Gavin Newsom has touted healthcare as a key aspect of his administration, framing it as a universal right for Californians. Early in his tenure, he signed an executive order directing the creation of a blueprint for a single-payer healthcare system, signaling his commitment to broad reforms. While the single-payer plan remains unfulfilled, Newsom has expanded Medi-Cal coverage to undocumented residents under the age of 26 and, later, to those over 50, positioning California as a national leader in inclusivity.

Newsom also launched CalRx, a program aimed at reducing prescription drug costs by negotiating lower prices for generic medications. His administration partnered with pharmaceutical companies to produce affordable naloxone (Narcan), a life-saving drug that reverses opioid overdoses. These efforts were hailed as progressive strides toward improving public health, though critics pointed to the logistical challenges and questioned whether the savings truly offset the high costs borne by taxpayers.

Despite these reforms, California's healthcare system faces persistent challenges. Overburdened emergency rooms, long wait times for specialized care, and rising costs remain significant barriers for residents. Many Californians argue that Newsom's focus on expanding coverage has come at the expense of addressing systemic inefficiencies, leaving the infrastructure strained under the weight of additional demand.

Leadership During the COVID-19 Pandemic

Newsom's handling of the COVID-19 pandemic was one of the most consequential aspects of his governorship. In March 2020, California became the first state to issue a stay-at-home order. Newsom described the decision as "guided by science and data," aiming to mitigate the virus's spread and prevent hospitals from being overwhelmed. The state initially received praise for its proactive measures, including large-scale testing, vaccination efforts, and resource deployment.

However, prolonged lockdowns and shifting mandates soon sparked widespread frustration. California endured some of the nation's longest and strictest restrictions, leading to significant economic and social repercussions. Small businesses were hit particularly hard, with thousands forced to shut down permanently. School closures persisted far longer than in many other states, deepening educational disparities and leaving parents struggling to adapt to remote learning. Critics pointed to these outcomes as evidence of a one-size-fits-all approach that overlooked the needs of specific communities.

The defining controversy of Newsom's pandemic leadership came in November 2020 when he attended a birthday party at the exclusive French Laundry restaurant in Napa Valley. The dinner, held in a private room, was for a close friend and political adviser. Newsom was photographed dining indoors, maskless, with a group of over a dozen people—directly contradicting his administration's public health guidelines that discouraged gatherings of more than three households.

The French Laundry scandal quickly became a symbol of political hypocrisy. At the time, Californians were being urged to cancel Thanksgiving plans, avoid social gatherings, and even miss the funerals of loved ones. Restaurants across the state faced severe restrictions, with many owners expressing outrage at the apparent double standard. Adding to the public backlash, the restaurant itself is synonymous with wealth and exclusivity, charging hundreds of dollars per plate—a stark contrast to the struggles faced by many Californians during the pandemic.

Newsom initially dismissed the criticism but later issued a public apology, calling the decision "a mistake" and acknowledging the damage it caused to public trust. He stated, "I need to practice what I preach, and I failed to do that. I let you down, and I will learn from this mistake." Despite the apology, the incident left a lasting stain on his leadership, fueling recall efforts and providing political ammunition for his opponents.

Addressing the Drug Overdose Crisis

The drug overdose crisis has emerged as a significant challenge during Newsom's tenure. In 2022, California recorded more than 10,000 overdose deaths, the highest total of any state, with synthetic opioids like fentanyl accounting for the majority of fatalities. The state's efforts to combat the crisis have included distributing free naloxone to first responders and community organizations, expanding treatment programs, and targeting illicit drug networks.

While California's overdose death rate remains lower than that of states like West Virginia, the sheer volume of fatalities underscores the gravity of the problem. Critics argue that the state's response has been inadequate, with insufficient resources devoted to prevention and long-term recovery programs. Newsom's supporters contend that the administration has made significant strides, particularly in making life-saving medications more accessible, but acknowledge that more work is needed to address the root causes of addiction.

A Polarizing Legacy

Newsom's healthcare policies and pandemic leadership highlight the complexities of governing in times of crisis. His progressive reforms and decisive actions have garnered praise from some, but his missteps—most notably the French Laundry incident—have fueled criticism and raised questions about his judgment. As California continues to grapple with healthcare challenges, drug addiction, and the fallout from the pandemic, Newsom's tenure offers a nuanced portrait of leadership under pressure.

Housing Affordability and Homelessness

Governor Gavin Newsom has made housing a central focus of his administration, framing California's affordability crisis as one of the most urgent issues facing the state. His tenure has seen numerous initiatives aimed at increasing the supply of affordable housing and addressing systemic barriers to construction.

- Bipartisan Housing Legislation: Newsom signed into law a $2.2 billion housing package to develop permanent supportive housing, particularly for veterans and individuals with mental health or substance use disorders. The legislation included measures to streamline zoning processes and hold local governments accountable for meeting housing targets.
- Homekey Initiative: The Homekey program was launched to acquire and convert underutilized buildings, such as hotels, into affordable housing. As of 2024, the program has added thousands of units to the state's housing stock, but demand continues to outpace supply.
- Streamlining Construction: Newsom's administration enacted policies aimed at cutting red tape for housing construction, including fast-tracking affordable housing projects and allowing for higher-density zoning in certain urban areas.

Despite these efforts, the cost of living in California remains the highest in the nation, with median home prices exceeding $700,000—more than double the national average. Renters fare no better, with median rents in metropolitan areas like San Francisco, Los Angeles, and San Diego hovering above $2,500 per month. For many, these costs make homeownership an unattainable dream and rent a constant financial strain.

The high cost of living, combined with the state's onerous taxes and rising crime rates, has led to a mass exodus from California in recent years. According to data from the U.S. Census Bureau, over 700,000 people left California between 2020 and 2022. The state has consistently seen more residents moving out than moving in, with many opting for states like Texas, Florida, and Arizona, where the cost of living is significantly lower. In fact, a 2021 study by the California Policy Center found that nearly half a million residents left the state in 2020 alone, and this trend shows no sign of slowing down. High taxes, limited housing options, and the increasing difficulty of achieving homeownership are driving this migration, particularly among middle-class families and retirees. This outflow of residents not only impacts California's tax base but also raises concerns about the future sustainability of its economy, as businesses and skilled workers seek more affordable living conditions elsewhere.

Homelessness: Rising Numbers Amid Record Spending

California's homelessness crisis has become one of the most visible and persistent challenges of Newsom's governorship. By 2023, the state's homeless population exceeded 181,000, the largest in the nation and accounting for over 30% of the U.S. total. While homelessness is a complex issue influenced by factors such as mental health, addiction, and income inequality, critics argue that state policies have exacerbated the problem.

- **Massive Spending with Mixed Results:** Since taking office, Newsom's administration has allocated over $24 billion toward combating homelessness, with approximately $15 billion spent during the COVID-19 pandemic alone. This equates to about $160,000 per unhoused person based on 2019 figures. However, homelessness has continued to rise, sparking debates about the efficacy of these expenditures.

- Focus on Temporary Solutions: Programs like Project Roomkey and Homekey have been lauded for providing temporary shelter but criticized for failing to offer long-term solutions. Critics contend that these initiatives focus too heavily on stopgap measures without addressing root causes, such as the lack of affordable housing and inadequate mental health services.

Decline in Quality of Life

The combined housing and homelessness crises have significantly affected the quality of life in California, leading to an increase in poverty, economic insecurity, and public health challenges.

- Housing-Related Poverty: Under the Supplemental Poverty Measure, which accounts for housing costs, California has the highest poverty rate in the nation at 13.2%. Rising housing costs are a primary driver, pushing families into precarious financial situations.
- Homeless Encampments: Major cities like Los Angeles, San Francisco, and Oakland have seen a proliferation of homeless encampments, often located in public spaces such as parks, sidewalks, and freeway underpasses. These encampments contribute to public safety and sanitation concerns, with local governments spending millions annually on clean-up efforts.
- Impact on Older Adults: A growing number of Californians over the age of 50 are experiencing homelessness for the first time, often due to a single financial setback or the inability to keep up with rising rents. This trend places additional strain on healthcare systems and social services.

If you ever question the declining quality of life in California, consider googling the "San Francisco Poop Map." The San

Francisco Poop Map underscores the extreme degradation of public spaces in the city, as it grapples with the growing homelessness crisis and an overwhelmed sanitation system. According to recent reports, over 30,000 incidents of public defecation have been reported annually, with the numbers continuing to rise. The issue is particularly prevalent in areas like the Tenderloin, South of Market, and the Mission District, where residents and visitors alike are often confronted with human waste on the streets. This growing problem has highlighted the serious public health concerns and the inability of the city to maintain even basic sanitation services in high-density, lower-income areas.

Despite being one of the most expensive places to live in the world, with median home prices topping $1.4 million and average rents in neighborhoods like South of Market exceeding $3,000 per month, San Francisco has failed to provide adequate solutions for its most pressing issues. The costs of living are skyrocketing, yet the city's infrastructure is struggling to keep up. Basic sanitation and waste removal services have not been able to meet the needs of a growing population, particularly in neighborhoods that are already facing severe housing shortages. The result is a stark disconnect between the high prices that residents are forced to pay and the increasingly unlivable conditions they must contend with.

The San Francisco Poop Map provides a chilling visual representation of this crisis, showing thousands of reported instances of public defecation across the city. The map illustrates how pervasive the issue has become, with major public spaces, sidewalks, and even business districts being affected. This widespread problem highlights the failure of the city's leadership to address both the homelessness crisis and the lack of public infrastructure to support the growing number of people who live on the streets. In a city where residents are paying some of the highest prices for real estate in the nation, the growing problem of human waste on the streets speaks volumes about the declining quality of life and the inability of San Francisco to provide a clean, safe environment for all its residents.

Criticism and Debate

Newsom's policies have drawn sharp criticism from various quarters. Some argue that the state's strict zoning and regulatory requirements continue to stifle housing development, even as billions are spent on homelessness programs. Others point to the disconnect between spending and outcomes, questioning whether funds are being used efficiently. Proponents of Newsom's approach argue that the scale of California's housing and homelessness crises requires time to address and that his initiatives represent progress in tackling systemic issues.

Personal Scandals

Sleeping with his friend's wife

In 2007, Gavin Newsom found himself at the center of a scandal that raised serious questions about his judgment and personal ethics. Newsom admitted to having an affair with Ruby Rippey-Tourk, who was not only his appointments secretary but also the wife of Alex Tourk, his close friend and campaign manager. The revelation sent shockwaves through San Francisco's political scene, as Tourk, feeling betrayed, immediately resigned from his role. The scandal was particularly damaging because it involved not just a breach of professional boundaries but also a profound personal betrayal. It highlighted Newsom's willingness to blur ethical lines in ways that undermined both his leadership and the trust of those closest to him.

This incident exemplifies a recurring theme in Newsom's career: poor judgment in moments of personal and political significance. His decision to engage in a relationship that jeopardized his professional team and betrayed a close friend reflects a pattern of prioritizing personal desires over ethical considerations. While Newsom publicly apologized for his actions and admitted it was a "terrible mistake," critics argue that the affair speaks to a broader lack of foresight and responsibility in his decision-making. This scandal, alongside others, has contributed to a narrative that Newsom's leadership style is often marred by impulsive and self-serving choices, raising concerns about his capacity to govern with the integrity and prudence expected of a leader.

French Laundry

The French Laundry incident remains one of the most notorious examples of Gavin Newsom's perceived hypocrisy during his tenure as governor. In November 2020, at the height of the COVID-19 pandemic, Newsom attended a birthday dinner for a political adviser at The French Laundry, a Michelin-starred restaurant in Napa Valley. The gathering included over a dozen guests from multiple households, flouting the strict guidelines his own administration had implemented, which prohibited gatherings of more than three households and strongly discouraged indoor dining. Photos of the maskless dinner quickly circulated, showing Newsom and others seated closely together in a private room, oblivious to the restrictions affecting millions of Californians. The imagery of extravagance during a time of collective sacrifice only amplified the backlash, with many viewing the incident as emblematic of a "rules for thee, but not for me" attitude.

The fallout from the scandal was swift and severe. Californians, already frustrated by prolonged lockdowns and economic hardship, saw the incident as a betrayal of public trust. Restaurant owners, who had been forced to shut their doors or operate under strict limitations, voiced outrage at what they saw as a double standard. Newsom later apologized, calling his attendance a "bad mistake," but the damage to his credibility lingered. For critics, the incident reinforced a pattern of poor judgment and tone-deaf decision-making that undermined his leadership during a time of crisis. The French Laundry dinner remains a focal point for those questioning Newsom's ability to lead with fairness and integrity, particularly when it comes to abiding by the same standards he enforces on others.

Getting under-aged girls drunk

Gavin Newsom's relationship with 19-year-old model Brittanie Mountz, following his divorce from Kimberly Guilfoyle, attracted significant controversy, primarily due to allegations of underage drinking during their time together. Newsom, then 39 and serving as the mayor of San Francisco, frequently took Mountz to upscale bars and nightlife venues, where reports surfaced that she had been seen consuming alcohol despite being under the legal drinking age. These allegations raised serious concerns about Newsom's judgment, as his decision to engage in such a relationship not only sparked ethical questions but also brought his personal choices into conflict with the law. The situation was further complicated by his prominent public role, where he was expected to uphold a standard of conduct befitting the city's leader.

Critics argued that this relationship underscored a troubling lack of discretion and responsibility, particularly as Newsom sought to present himself as a progressive and principled political figure. While the relationship itself was legal, his association with underage drinking exposed him to accusations of enabling or condoning behavior that contradicted his responsibilities as a public official. The media frenzy surrounding the relationship detracted from his mayoral duties and cast a shadow over his initiatives. For many, the controversy served as yet another example of Newsom's recurring pattern of prioritizing personal indulgence over accountability and foresight, leaving questions about his ability to lead with integrity.

Hiding Donations

In 2024, Gavin Newsom faced backlash and a $13,000 fine for failing to disclose 18 charitable donations made on his behalf, as mandated by California state law. One of the most notable contributions came from T-Mobile, raising concerns about potential conflicts of interest. State regulations require elected officials to report such donations promptly to ensure transparency and accountability, yet Newsom's delays in reporting these contributions sparked debates about his commitment to ethical governance. Observers questioned whether this oversight reflected deeper issues within his administration's adherence to legal and ethical standards.

This lapse in reporting prompted accusations of negligence, with many suggesting it revealed a pattern of carelessness in financial disclosures. Others speculated about the potential influence of major donors like T-Mobile on state policy decisions, adding fuel to the controversy. While Newsom's team claimed the omissions were unintentional, the episode raised broader concerns about trust and transparency in his administration. For some, the incident served as a reminder of the importance of rigorous oversight and the need for public officials to uphold the highest ethical standards to maintain confidence in their leadership.

Covid Hypocrisy

Gavin Newsom's handling of California's COVID-19 restrictions has been marred by a series of incidents that collectively paint a picture of inconsistent adherence to the very protocols he mandated for the public. One such controversy arose when Newsom was seen dining indoors at a Panera Bread without a mask, despite California's strict regulations prohibiting indoor dining and requiring face coverings in public spaces. The incident drew immediate criticism, with many accusing him of holding himself to a different standard than the millions of Californians who had to abide by the state's restrictive policies. This lapse in judgment not only undermined the credibility of his public health directives but also fueled frustration among residents already weary of the pandemic's toll on daily life.

Adding to the perception of hypocrisy was Newsom's appearance at an NFL game in a luxury suite, where he was photographed maskless alongside other guests. This incident came at a time when his administration was strongly advocating for mask-wearing in all indoor and crowded outdoor settings. The opulence of the setting—a private suite at a high-profile event—further exacerbated public resentment, as small business owners and workers were still grappling with the fallout from prolonged restrictions. Critics seized on the imagery, portraying Newsom as out of touch with the struggles of ordinary Californians while flouting the very rules he had emphasized as essential for public safety.

The controversy extended to his family, when it was revealed that Newsom's children attended a summer camp where mask-wearing was not enforced, in direct violation of state guidelines. While Newsom claimed that the family was unaware of the camp's lax policies and withdrew his children as soon as it was brought to their attention, the damage to his reputation was already done. For many, the incident epitomized a lack of accountability and consistency in applying pandemic protocols. Parents who had adhered to strict masking and distancing rules for their own children felt particularly incensed, viewing the situation as yet another example of a double standard.

Together, these incidents underscored a recurring pattern in Newsom's leadership during the pandemic: an ability to impose strict regulations on the public while failing to uphold those same standards in his personal and professional life. While Newsom repeatedly defended his administration's decisions as necessary to protect public health, these missteps eroded trust and provided ammunition for his critics. The perception of hypocrisy not only damaged his credibility but also amplified broader frustrations with California's handling of the pandemic, leaving many to question whether the sacrifices demanded of residents were being shared equally by their leaders.

State Funds for Personal Use

Gavin Newsom has faced persistent allegations that he used state funds for personal expenses, a controversy that has cast a shadow over his reputation for fiscal accountability. Reports surfaced suggesting that state resources were misused to cover items such as alcohol, luxury goods, and other personal indulgences. Although investigations into these claims did not lead to formal charges, the allegations raised questions about Newsom's judgment and the oversight within his administration. Critics pointed to the perceived disconnect between his public messaging on fiscal responsibility and these accusations, which painted a different picture of his handling of taxpayer money.

One particularly contentious example involved claims that Newsom expensed high-end wine purchases for events not clearly tied to state business. These allegations were compounded by reports of excessive spending on luxury accommodations during official travel, further fueling the narrative that he prioritized personal comfort over public accountability. While Newsom's team maintained that all expenses were appropriate and within the bounds of state regulations, the lack of transparency surrounding the expenditures left room for speculation and criticism.

These allegations struck a chord with Californians already burdened by rising taxes and the state's high cost of living. For many, the idea that public funds could be used for personal luxuries during a time of economic hardship felt like a betrayal of trust. Although no charges were filed, the controversy added to a broader perception of entitlement and privilege within Newsom's leadership style, reinforcing the narrative that he often fails to lead by example when it comes to ethical governance and fiscal restraint.

Mismanagement of Unemployment Benefits

Under Governor Gavin Newsom's administration, the California Employment Development Department (EDD) encountered a significant fraud scandal during the COVID-19 pandemic, resulting in the disbursement of billions of dollars in fraudulent unemployment claims. In January 2021, EDD officials acknowledged that approximately $11 billion had been paid to fraudulent claimants, with an additional $19 billion in claims under investigation for potential fraud. This situation highlighted substantial deficiencies in the state's oversight mechanisms and raised concerns about the administration's capacity to manage the surge in unemployment claims during the crisis.

The majority of the fraudulent payments were linked to the federal Pandemic Unemployment Assistance (PUA) program, which was particularly susceptible to exploitation. The EDD estimated that 9.7% of payments made were fraudulent, with 95% of these fraudulent claims associated with the PUA program. The department also reported that it had identified and prevented up to $60 billion in fraudulent claims before disbursement. Despite these preventive measures, the substantial amount of funds lost to fraud underscored significant vulnerabilities within the system.

The repercussions of this mismanagement extended beyond financial losses. By the summer of 2021, California owed $23 billion to the federal government for unemployment benefits paid during the pandemic, accounting for 43% of all unemployment debt owed by 13 states at that time. This debt was largely due to longstanding underfunding and the state's high unemployment rate during the pandemic, rather than the fraudulent claims themselves. The combination of massive fraud and escalating debt intensified scrutiny of Governor Newsom's leadership and the effectiveness of his administration's response to the unprecedented challenges posed by the pandemic.

Wildfire Mismanagement

Under Governor Gavin Newsom's administration, California's wildfire prevention efforts have faced significant criticism due to alleged mismanagement of allocated funds, resulting in devastating fires and raising concerns about the state's preparedness. In 2021, it was revealed that fire prevention work was vastly overstated, with the administration claiming that 90,000 acres had been treated across priority projects. However, state data indicated that only about 11,399 acres were actually addressed, just 13% of the reported figure. This discrepancy highlighted a gap between what was promised and what was delivered, casting doubt on the administration's commitment to mitigating wildfire risks.

Adding to the issue, the state reduced Cal Fire's wildfire prevention budget by $150 million, a decision that critics argue left California more vulnerable. The consequences were catastrophic during the 2020 fire season, which became the worst in the state's history. Over 4.3 million acres burned, thousands of homes were destroyed, and 33 lives were lost. The scale of the devastation underscored the severe human and economic toll of these disasters, which disproportionately affected rural and vulnerable communities across the state.

The fires left many residents homeless and displaced, leading to long-term financial and emotional hardships. Rebuilding efforts required significant financial investment, with California allocating $536 million for wildfire mitigation and forest management in 2021 alone. These funds were critical for recovery and for bolstering future resilience, but the delayed and reactive nature of the investments called into question the state's ability to prioritize prevention over emergency response.

Together, the mismanagement of wildfire prevention funds and the resulting damage to lives and property have amplified scrutiny of Governor Newsom's leadership. Critics argue that inadequate preparation, combined with an overemphasis on optics over action, exacerbated the crisis and left California ill-equipped to handle one of its most persistent threats. This controversy highlights the need for transparency, adequate funding, and proactive management to safeguard the state from the increasing risks posed by wildfires.

Conflict of Interest in Business Deals

Gavin Newsom has faced ongoing scrutiny over potential conflicts of interest linked to his personal investments and the companies that have benefited from state and city contracts during his time in office. A key example of this controversy revolves around his involvement with the PlumpJack Group, a wine and hospitality company he co-founded in 1992 with funding from wealthy individuals, including prominent investors in the real estate and entertainment industries. Newsom maintained ownership in the company while serving as mayor of San Francisco and later as governor. Reports suggested that some of the PlumpJack Group's business dealings were influenced by Newsom's political position. For example, PlumpJack received millions in loans from the city of San Francisco during his tenure as mayor, despite the company having strong ties to Newsom's personal network of investors. The city's investments in PlumpJack properties raised eyebrows, with critics questioning whether Newsom's position as mayor could have swayed the city's financial decisions.

In addition to these local ties, Newsom's relationships with influential figures, such as the Getty family, further raised concerns about preferential treatment. The Gettys were major investors in PlumpJack, and their connections within both the political and business worlds prompted fears that Newsom's policies could have been shaped to benefit his personal financial interests. One instance involved a luxury hotel project supported by both the city and state, where Newsom's involvement in securing state-backed loans for the project drew allegations of cronyism. While Newsom and his supporters maintained that all business deals were above board, the perception of a conflict of interest persisted, especially as public records indicated that investments linked to his personal network received favorable treatment in the form of tax incentives, grants, and development approvals.

This situation contributed to broader concerns about the influence of business interests in political decision-making and fueled calls for stronger ethics reforms. The failure to fully disclose these relationships left some voters questioning whether Newsom was able to fully separate his political duties from his financial interests. Critics argued that such connections could undermine public trust in the fairness and transparency of his governance.

Campaign Finance Violations

Gavin Newsom faced significant controversy over campaign finance violations during his 2018 campaign for governor, particularly for knowingly accepting donations that exceeded California's legal limits. Under state law, individual donations to gubernatorial campaigns are capped at $29,200 per person. However, Newsom's campaign was found to have accepted multiple donations above this threshold from various high-profile donors, including corporate entities and wealthy individuals. One of the most notable violations involved a $50,000 donation from a real estate developer, which was well above the legal limit. These violations were brought to light by the California Fair Political Practices Commission (FPPC), which investigated the donations and ultimately imposed fines on Newsom's campaign for exceeding contribution limits.

In addition to the $50,000 donation, Newsom's campaign committee also accepted large contributions from other sources, including a $30,000 donation from the California State Association of Electrical Workers and additional funds from various business leaders and PACs with interests in state policy. Critics argued that these large donations undermined the integrity of Newsom's campaign, giving the appearance that corporate interests could potentially influence his policy decisions. Although the donations were later refunded, the fact that they were knowingly accepted raised concerns about the transparency and ethical practices surrounding Newsom's fundraising operations.

Despite the minor fines imposed by the FPPC—totaling $15,000 for these violations—the controversy raised important questions about the role of big money in California politics. It highlighted the difficulty of enforcing campaign finance laws, which often allow for technical violations to go unnoticed or unpunished unless exposed. The incident also added to the growing perception that Newsom's ties to wealthy donors and corporate interests may have compromised his public image as a progressive leader, causing further scrutiny of his ability to govern independently from those who financially supported his campaign.

Misleading COVID-19 Statistics

Governor Gavin Newsom's handling of COVID-19 data during the pandemic has been criticized for alleged manipulation of statistics to justify extended lockdowns and stringent public health measures. Throughout the pandemic, Newsom's administration faced accusations of presenting misleading or incomplete data, which critics argue was used to justify prolonged restrictions that hurt small businesses and the broader economy. One of the most controversial issues involved the state's tracking system for COVID-19 cases and deaths, with concerns that the data was adjusted or selectively reported to create a narrative that supported Newsom's policies.

In late 2020, Newsom's administration came under fire for reporting inflated numbers of cases and deaths in certain regions, leading to confusion and fear among the public. For example, in December 2020, a statistical error was discovered in the state's reporting system, which resulted in the inclusion of previously reported cases in the total count. This error led to an artificially inflated spike in cases, which Newsom used to justify a new round of stay-at-home orders. The error was later corrected, but the incident fueled suspicions that the state was overstating the severity of the situation to maintain a narrative of crisis. Newsom's team later explained that the error was a result of a technical glitch, but the incident raised concerns about the transparency and accuracy of data being used to enforce harsh public health policies.

Additionally, the state's inconsistent reporting of death tolls further damaged public trust. In some instances, COVID-19-related deaths were classified without clear evidence of the virus being the primary cause of death, inflating the actual fatality count. By mid-2021, it was reported that California had one of the highest total numbers of COVID-19 deaths, but some experts questioned the accuracy of the figures, pointing out that deaths related to other causes were sometimes categorized as COVID-19-related in the state's database. Critics argued that Newsom's administration, in its push to extend emergency powers and lockdown measures, might have over-emphasized data points that justified stricter controls, without sufficiently considering the broader context or potential inaccuracies in reporting.

The manipulation of COVID-19 data was not just limited to case and death statistics. In 2020, Newsom also faced criticism for his handling of test positivity rates. The state introduced a new system for tracking the spread of the virus, using color-coded tiers to determine which counties could reopen. However, many counties, particularly those with low population densities, were placed in the most restrictive tiers despite having low positivity rates. This led to accusations that Newsom's team was skewing the metrics to prolong shutdowns in economically vulnerable regions. By the time California began loosening restrictions in mid-2021, many businesses and schools had already suffered from months of economically devastating measures, and some questioned whether the restrictions were based on accurate, fair, and transparent data or on political motives to control the situation through extended executive authority.

Personal Use of Campaign Funds

Governor Gavin Newsom has faced allegations of improperly using campaign funds for personal expenses, a controversy that raised questions about his ethical standards and transparency in political fundraising. During his 2018 gubernatorial campaign, investigations revealed that Newsom used campaign funds for expenditures that were not directly related to his political activities, including personal vacations, luxury items, and other expenses that many saw as benefiting his private lifestyle. While Newsom's campaign committee insisted that all expenditures were legitimate and within the bounds of the law, the nature of some of these purchases led to public outcry and sparked an ethics investigation.

One of the most notable instances involved a trip to the French Laundry, the same upscale restaurant that later became the center of controversy during the COVID-19 pandemic. It was reported that Newsom's campaign paid for the expenses surrounding this trip, which critics argued was a misuse of funds intended for political purposes. In addition to the French Laundry incident, Newsom's campaign was found to have paid for personal items such as hotel stays and meals at high-end restaurants, raising questions about whether these expenses were justified as campaign-related. While the expenditures were relatively small compared to the total funds raised, they underscored a broader concern about transparency and accountability in the handling of political donations.

The California Fair Political Practices Commission (FPPC) reviewed these allegations and ultimately imposed a fine on Newsom's campaign for misusing funds. The fine, though not large, served as a reminder of the potential for abuse in campaign finance, especially when funds are raised through extensive donations from corporations, unions, and wealthy individuals. The scandal contributed to the narrative that Newsom, despite his progressive image, was not immune to the same ethical lapses that often plague politicians involved in high-stakes campaigns. Critics argued that the personal use of campaign funds not only undermined public trust but also highlighted the need for stricter regulations and oversight in the political fundraising process.

As potential voters consider Gavin Newsom in the lead-up to the 2028 presidential election, it's crucial to evaluate not just his policy achievements, but also the controversies that have followed him throughout his political career. From personal scandals and campaign finance violations to mismanagement of state resources and accusations of misleading the public, Newsom's record raises important questions about his judgment, transparency, and ethical standards. While he has championed progressive causes in California, these controversies serve as a reminder of the potential risks of leadership that has been marred by questionable decisions and inconsistent actions. As the nation looks ahead, voters will need to carefully weigh both his accomplishments and his flaws in determining whether he is truly the leader they want for the future.

Chapter 4

Gavin Newsom's Radical Transgenderism

Gavin Newsom has firmly positioned himself as a staunch advocate for transgender rights, championing policies that he says extend far beyond simple anti-discrimination measures. His stance on transgenderism, which has shaped much of his political career in California, reflects his broader progressive agenda that pushes for societal transformation. While his supporters hail him as a leader of inclusivity and equality, his policies have sparked significant opposition, particularly among Californians who see his approach as a direct assault on traditional values and biological realities.

Newsom's actions in California have made the state a battleground for transgender activism, as he has supported laws that grant transgender individuals the right to access gender-specific facilities, participate in sports, and receive medical treatments regardless of biological sex. He has signed multiple bills into law that prioritize the rights of transgender people over the rights of others, such as California's Senate Bill 132, which allows prisoners to be housed according to their gender identity, regardless of their biological sex. While these policies are presented as a necessary step towards equality and fairness, many Californians argue that they undermine common sense, parental rights, and the safety of women and children.

Moreover, Newsom's push to make California a sanctuary state for transgender individuals has garnered national attention. He has signed executive orders and legislation that not only shield transgender minors from parental consent in medical decisions but also prevent law enforcement from cooperating with out-of-state requests for those seeking transgender medical procedures. To clarify, this means that if a child runs away to get irreversible surgeries or hormones, the state of California will not help parents intervene.

Newsom has publicly advocated for unrestricted access to hormone therapies and gender-affirming surgeries, regardless of age or parental consent. For many Californians, this represents a troubling erosion of parental rights and the protection of children, particularly in the context of medical interventions that can have irreversible consequences.

Newsom's support for transgender individuals extends into the realm of public education, where he has endorsed policies that allow children to participate in sports based on their gender identity, rather than their biological sex. California became one of the first states to pass legislation that ensures transgender students can compete in sports teams that match their gender identity, a policy that critics argue compromises fairness in women's sports. Newsom's backing of such policies has been celebrated by some, but for conservatives, it raises serious concerns about the erosion of biological distinctions and the undermining of fair competition.

This chapter will explore Gavin Newsom's stance on transgenderism in detail, examining his policies, public statements, and the implications they have on California and the nation as a whole. It will also address the growing divide between Newsom's vision of inclusivity and the concerns of many who believe that such policies are not only misguided but dangerous. For some Californians, Newsom's support for transgenderism is a symptom of a larger issue: the progressive agenda that seeks to redefine basic biological truths and impose these redefinitions on society at large.

The Implications of Senate Bill 132 and Newsom's Approach to Transgender Rights

Governor Gavin Newsom's support for transgender rights has been one of the defining elements of his leadership in California. One of the most controversial actions in his record on transgender issues was his signing of Senate Bill 132 into law in 2019. This bill allows transgender inmates to be housed in California state prisons according to their gender identity rather than their biological sex. While Newsom framed the bill as a "common-sense solution" to ensure transgender individuals have a safe and dignified experience in California's prison system, many critics argue that this policy has led to a host of unforeseen and often damaging consequences. This bill has sparked outrage from those with traditional values, victims' rights advocates, and even some within the LGBTQ+ community, who question whether this policy puts women at risk and undermines the integrity of the correctional system.

The Passage of Senate Bill 132

SB 132 was introduced by State Senator Scott Wiener (D-San Francisco) and passed through the California legislature with Newsom's strong backing. The bill allows transgender individuals to request placement in a prison facility based on their gender identity, rather than the sex they were assigned at birth. In other words, a man convicted with kidnapping, beating, and raping women now has the right to be housed in a prison full of women, so long as he declares that he is one. Supporters of the bill, including Newsom, argued that it was necessary to protect the safety and dignity of transgender prisoners, who historically have been housed according to their biological sex and have faced high rates of harassment, assault, and discrimination in correctional facilities. Newsom, in his statement after signing the bill into law, emphasized that transgender prisoners should have the right to live in an environment that respects their gender identity. He called the law a "common-sense solution" to protect transgender inmates from abuse and to ensure they were treated with dignity.

The Unintended Consequences

While Newsom and his supporters praised the bill as a step forward for transgender rights, critics warned of the potential dangers and unintended consequences of housing transgender women (biological males) in women's prisons. The law immediately raised concerns about the safety and fairness of such a policy, especially for the women housed in California's correctional facilities.

1. Increased Risk to Female Inmates
   One of the most significant concerns about SB 132 is the potential risk it poses to female inmates. Critics argue that placing male-born prisoners, even those who identify as female, in women's prisons creates an inherent safety risk for female inmates. Transgender women, despite identifying as female, often retain male anatomy, including penises, which in these settings leads to instances of sexual abuse, intimidation, and violence in female correctional facilities.

For example, in 2021, California prison officials confirmed that several transgender women were placed in women's prisons under SB 132. According to reports, one such transgender woman was convicted of violent crimes against women, including rape, prior to transitioning. Even in California, many argue that housing individuals with violent criminal backgrounds in women's prisons, regardless of their gender identity, undermines the safety of vulnerable populations.

Furthermore, California's Department of Corrections and Rehabilitation (CDCR) reported a significant increase in the number of complaints from female inmates regarding inappropriate behavior and assault by transgender women placed in women's facilities. Women in California prisons already face a disproportionate level of abuse and violence. According to a 2019 report by the Bureau of Justice Statistics, approximately 1 in 10 women in prison report experiencing sexual abuse by staff or other inmates. Critics argue that SB 132 exacerbates these issues by allowing for the possibility of more male-bodied individuals, who may have prior convictions for violent or sexual crimes, being placed in women's facilities.

2. The Problem of Mismatched Housing Based on Gender Identity

   Another criticism of SB 132 is that it ignores the basic biological reality that not all transgender women undergo full gender-affirming surgeries or medical treatments. Many transgender women still have male genitalia and physical characteristics that could make it difficult for women in prison to feel safe and comfortable. The idea of a biological male, regardless of their gender identity, sharing living quarters with female prisoners can feel inherently threatening to women who have often faced violence at the hands of men prior to their incarceration.

This issue has become even more pronounced in California prisons where sexual misconduct remains a significant problem. In 2020, a Los Angeles Times investigation found that nearly half of female inmates in California prisons had reported being victims of sexual violence. The presence of male criminals in women's facilities only adds to the complexities surrounding this already troubling issue. Critics believe that Newsom's policy fails to recognize the rights of female prisoners who feel that their safety and dignity are compromised by the presence of men.

3. The Impact on Correctional Staff
   In addition to the risks faced by female inmates,
   Newsom's approach has also raised concerns among
   correctional staff, who are tasked with managing facilities
   with increasingly complex populations. Many
   correctional officers have expressed frustration with the
   lack of clear guidelines regarding the housing and
   treatment of both men and women. Critics argue that
   Newsom's policy has created additional challenges for
   staff, who are now tasked with navigating situations
   where inmates' gender identity may not align with their
   biological sex. This has led to confusion and difficulties
   in managing prison populations, as well as concerns over
   the potential for lawsuits and liability issues in cases of
   abuse or assault.

4. Legal Challenges and Public Backlash
   The passage of SB 132 and Newsom's support for it have
   led to multiple legal challenges and public backlash. In
   2020, several groups, including women's advocacy
   organizations, filed lawsuits against the California prison
   system, arguing that the new law violated the
   constitutional rights of female inmates. The Pacific Legal
   Foundation, a conservative legal organization, called the
   law an "unconstitutional infringement" on the rights of
   women in prison, arguing that the state's primary duty is
   to ensure the safety and well-being of all inmates,
   particularly vulnerable populations such as women.

This legal pushback is further complicated by the growing
national debate over transgender rights and how they intersect
with other protected classes, including women's rights. Some of
Newsom's critics argue that his push for transgender rights has
created a conflict with the rights of women, especially in spaces
that are designed for female-only populations, such as prisons and
sports. They argue that the law disproportionately benefits men

who want to escape the more dangerous male prisons, while undermining the safety, privacy, and rights of women, who are already vulnerable within the correctional system.

5. The Broader Impact of Newsom's Policy
   Beyond the immediate implications of SB 132 in California prisons, Newsom's stance on transgender rights represents a broader societal shift toward policies that many conservatives view as overly accommodating to transgender individuals at the expense of other groups. Supporters of the bill, including Newsom, argue that it is necessary to protect the human dignity of men who think they are women, and vice versa, particularly those who have faced discrimination and violence. However, some Californians contend that such policies undermine common-sense principles of fairness, safety, and biological reality.

There have been several cases in California where transgender individuals, particularly transgender women (biological males who identify as female), have been involved in criminal activities while incarcerated. These cases have raised concerns about the implications of California's policies allowing transgender prisoners to be housed according to their gender identity, rather than their biological sex. Here are a few notable incidents that have sparked significant media attention and public debate:

1. The Case of "Shane" (Transgender Woman in Women's Prisons)

One of the most well-known cases involved Shane, a man who declared he was a woman who was housed in a women's prison despite having a history of violent offenses committed before transitioning. In 2016, Shane was placed in a women's facility after identifying as female. However, Shane's background as a male with a history of violent crimes—including convictions for rape and assault—raised questions about the safety and fairness of housing such individuals in women's prisons.

Despite her transition, Shane was a predator with a history of violence against women, and her placement in a women's facility raised concerns about the safety of the women she was housed with. Critics of California's policy argued that, while transgender individuals should have access to safe housing, the placement of individuals with violent criminal histories in women's prisons can lead to situations where biologically male individuals with histories of sexual assault are housed with vulnerable female inmates, leading to increased risk of assault and other forms of abuse.

2. "Kathy" (Transgender Woman Convicted of Murder)

Another example involves Kathy, a transgender woman serving time for murder. Kathy had committed a violent crime prior to transitioning and, under California's new policies, was housed in a women's facility. However, due to Kathy's violent criminal history, including an assaultive past, concerns arose about the appropriateness of housing someone with such a background in a women's prison. The concern here was similar—while men who believe they are women still deserve to be treated with dignity, there were obvious questions about the risks posed to incarcerated women when a history of violence and aggression was involved.

In most cases, advocates for the safety of women in prisons have argued that the criminal history of men who declare they are women does not matter when determining appropriate housing, because the simple inclusion of male criminals in women's prisons makes the female inmates less safe.

3. California's Prison System and the Overhaul in Housing Policies

The broader issue in California is related to the law signed by Governor Gavin Newsom in 2020 (Senate Bill 132), which allows transgender inmates to request to be housed in facilities that correspond with their gender identity. This law, which was touted as a step toward ensuring the safety and dignity of transgender individuals in prison, has led to several high-profile cases where transgender women (biologically male) with violent criminal histories were placed in women's facilities, leading to growing concerns about the safety of other inmates.

As of recent reports, approximately 300 transgender individuals have requested transfers to women's prisons under this law, and there are growing concerns about the safety implications, particularly in light of sexual assaults and violent behavior committed by some transgender women. These incidents have sparked debates about whether the policy is effective in balancing the safety of transgender prisoners and that of other incarcerated individuals, particularly women.

Transgender Rights and Healthcare: A Controversial Agenda

Governor Gavin Newsom's administration has played a leading role in expanding access to so-called healthcare for transgender individuals in California, pushing for policies that provide comprehensive gender-affirming care. His advocacy for transgender rights includes ensuring that transgender people, especially minors, have access to medical interventions such as hormone therapy and gender-affirming surgeries, which, according to Newsom, are necessary for individuals to live their lives "fully and authentically." While these policies are presented as progressive steps toward inclusion and equality, many traditional Californians, medical professionals, and ethicists are deeply concerned about the irreversible physical and psychological consequences of such treatments, especially when applied to vulnerable minors.

In 2019, Newsom's administration made headlines by expanding Medi-Cal, California's Medicaid program, to provide coverage for a wide range of transgender-related healthcare services, including hormone therapy, gender-affirming surgeries, and other medical procedures often associated with transitioning. These services are now available to anyone enrolled in Medi-Cal, regardless of income or age, as long as they meet the medical criteria for gender dysphoria.

Newsom's statement on transgender healthcare emphasizes that transgender individuals should have access to care that supports their gender identity. He argued that gender-affirming care is not just a luxury or an elective procedure, but a fundamental healthcare need for many transgender people, especially those who face mental health challenges related to gender dysphoria. In his own words, Newsom stated, "Transgender individuals deserve to have access to the health care that will allow them to live their lives fully and authentically. We need to ensure that we remove any barriers to care, especially for our most vulnerable communities." On the surface, this statement seems compassionate, advocating for healthcare equity, but the consequences of implementing such a policy are far more complex and troubling than Newsom acknowledges.

Hormone Therapy and Puberty Blockers: A Dangerous Precedent for Children

One of the most controversial aspects of Newsom's transgender healthcare policies is his push for hormone therapy and puberty blockers for minors. Puberty blockers are drugs that delay the onset of puberty, preventing the development of physical characteristics such as breasts in girls or facial hair in boys. These drugs, including lupron, are often prescribed to transgender minors to halt the natural puberty process and give them time to make decisions about whether they wish to pursue further gender-affirming treatments.

While Newsom and his supporters argue that these treatments are necessary to alleviate the suffering of transgender youth, critics argue that these interventions are irreversible and come with significant risks. Puberty blockers can lead to long-term health complications, including osteoporosis, fertility issues, and psychological side effects. Some studies have shown that children who undergo these treatments may suffer from reduced bone density, a concern that has prompted medical professionals to call for caution when administering puberty blockers to children. Additionally, hormone therapies, which are prescribed to help individuals transition to a different gender, carry their own risks, including heart disease, diabetes, and increased cancer risks.

Some Californians also raise the issue that these treatments are often administered to minors who may not fully understand the consequences of their decisions. While Newsom's policies are framed as compassionate and aimed at addressing gender dysphoria, they disregard the reality that many children and teenagers who experience gender confusion may outgrow it over time. Studies have shown that a significant percentage of children diagnosed with gender dysphoria do not continue to identify as transgender once they reach adulthood, raising questions about the wisdom of subjecting minors to permanent medical treatments. By expanding Medi-Cal coverage for gender-affirming care, Newsom's policies encourage parents and minors to make life-altering decisions before they are able to fully comprehend the long-term implications.

Gender-Affirming Surgeries: The Mutilation of Healthy Bodies

Another deeply controversial aspect of Newsom's support for transgender rights is his endorsement of gender-affirming surgeries for minors, which are covered under Medi-Cal. These surgeries include breast augmentation for trans women (biological males transitioning to females) and mastectomies for trans men (biological females transitioning to males). Genital reassignment surgery is also part of the gender-affirming care that Newsom supports, despite significant ethical concerns surrounding these procedures for minors.

The decision to undergo surgeries that alter healthy, functioning body parts is often irreversible and carries substantial risks. Mastectomies performed on young girls to remove their breasts—a procedure that many argue constitutes mutilation of healthy tissue—are typically done in an effort to align a person's physical appearance with their gender identity. Newsom has defended these surgeries, stating that they are part of a necessary and humane healthcare strategy to help transgender individuals feel comfortable in their own bodies. However, the psychological and physical costs of such drastic procedures are undeniable, and their long-term effects remain under-researched.

The decision to support such procedures for minors is not without serious ethical concerns. Adolescents, whose bodies and identities are still in flux, may not fully comprehend the ramifications of such surgeries. For example, a 2018 study by the American Academy of Pediatrics found that 60% of transgender youth report feeling regret or uncertainty about their decision to transition years after undergoing medical treatments or surgeries. Despite these studies, Newsom's policies push for access to these irreversible surgeries at a time when minors may not be equipped to understand the full consequences of altering their bodies permanently.

There is also the question of whether healthcare providers should have the authority to carry out such procedures on minors in the absence of a fully informed consent process. Californian parents argue that transgender youth often face immense pressure from social media, peer groups, and even political activists to pursue transitioning, and that these pressures can cloud their judgment. Transitioning minors, as seen in some studies, may not have the maturity to navigate the complexities of their identity and the ramifications of life-altering medical procedures. Yet, Newsom's administration has not only supported but actively expanded the availability of such treatments, positioning California as a sanctuary state for transgender youth seeking gender-affirming care.

Medi-Cal and the Expansion of Access

Medi-Cal's role in facilitating access to gender-affirming care has become a cornerstone of Newsom's policies aimed at advancing transgender rights in California. By extending full coverage for transgender-related healthcare services, Newsom ensures that all Californians, regardless of income, can access treatments such as hormone therapy, puberty blockers, and surgeries. While Newsom's administration argues that this is a step toward greater inclusivity and equity, it raises concerns about the long-term implications of using taxpayer dollars to fund treatments that critics consider to be medically unproven and potentially harmful.

Newsom's backing of Medi-Cal's coverage for gender-affirming care directly challenges the principles of medical ethics and informed consent. Many medical professionals argue that transitioning minors—especially those without the cognitive maturity to make fully informed decisions about their futures—is highly unethical. Critics also argue that expanding Medi-Cal to cover such treatments encourages doctors to provide services that may not align with long-term health and safety standards. For example, California Medical Association guidelines have advised caution when prescribing hormone therapy and surgeries for minors, yet Newsom's policies seem to disregard such concerns.

The Larger Social and Ethical Debate

Newsom's approach to transgender healthcare has sparked a broader ethical debate, not only within the medical community but also within the broader public discourse. While many liberals view his policies as necessary for advancing civil rights and inclusivity, conservatives argue that Newsom's approach is reckless and harmful, particularly to vulnerable minors. The question is not whether transgender individuals should have access to healthcare, but rather whether the specific treatments Newsom supports—such as irreversible surgeries and hormone therapies for minors—should be considered acceptable forms of care.

In Newsom's California, the pressure for conformity to gender-affirming treatment protocols has made it difficult to question the wisdom of transitioning minors. Those who raise concerns about the potential harms of such treatments—whether physical, psychological, or social—are often dismissed as transphobic or opposed to human rights. The growing number of detransitioners—individuals who regret their decision to transition—raises alarms that California's approach to transgender healthcare may be encouraging irreversible, life-altering decisions without fully understanding the long-term consequences.

The contrast between the legal age restrictions for activities like smoking, getting tattoos, and starting hormone therapy or puberty blockers highlights the deep inconsistencies in how society views the maturity of minors when it comes to making decisions about their bodies and long-term health. In California, the legal age to purchase tobacco products is 21, and individuals cannot legally get a tattoo without parental consent until they are 18. These laws exist to protect minors from making potentially harmful decisions—decisions that could have lasting consequences on their physical health, well-being, and future quality of life. But when it comes to irreversible medical treatments like puberty blockers and hormone therapy, children as young as 12 are allowed to begin undergoing treatments that have profound and permanent effects on their bodies and hormones. This inconsistency is not only troubling but also raises serious questions about whether society truly considers minors capable of making life-altering medical decisions.

Hormone therapy and puberty blockers are far more invasive and permanent than activities like smoking or getting a tattoo. Puberty blockers can delay the onset of puberty, and if continued, they can stunt natural growth and development, potentially causing long-term health problems like osteoporosis or fertility issues. Hormone therapy, whether it involves testosterone or estrogen, is even more drastic, as it can induce irreversible physical changes such as the growth of facial hair for girls or breast tissue for boys. These are decisions that can affect a child's ability to have biological children, their physical appearance, and their mental health for the rest of their lives. Yet, while society mandates that minors wait until they are 18 to make decisions about their tattoos or to smoke—both activities that, while harmful, do not fundamentally alter a person's biological makeup—medical professionals are legally allowed to administer treatments to children that permanently alter their bodies, with far-reaching consequences that many argue they are too young to fully understand.

This inconsistency is compounded by the fact that minors are not allowed to make other decisions that could have far less long-term impact on their lives without parental consent, such as voting or buying alcohol. Yet, in the case of puberty blockers and hormone therapy, minors are often making life-altering decisions with medical professionals' approval, sometimes with little oversight or emotional maturity to fully grasp the consequences. These stark contradictions should force us to question the wisdom of allowing young people to undergo treatments with lifelong implications while simultaneously denying them the ability to make less permanent, less consequential decisions on their own. When society sets an age of majority for other significant decisions, but then allows children to be chemically or physically altered without fully understanding the consequences, it raises the fundamental question: why are we allowing children to make permanent decisions about their bodies that we wouldn't allow them to make for far less impactful matters?

This disjointed approach reflects not only a failure to protect minors from potential harm but also an ideological commitment to advancing policies that prioritize progressive agendas over common sense and biological realities. It is a call to reexamine the balance between protecting vulnerable populations, like children, and pushing policies that impose irreversible changes without fully understanding the long-term effects on their lives. The contradiction is not just a matter of policy inconsistency—it is about making sure that minors are not subjected to decisions that they are too young, emotionally and intellectually, to fully comprehend.

Governor Gavin Newsom's policies on transgender healthcare have made California a beacon of progressive ideology on gender issues, but the consequences of these policies are highly controversial. His expansion of Medi-Cal to cover gender-affirming care, including hormone therapy and surgeries, has set a dangerous precedent for the rest of the nation, particularly regarding the treatment of minors. Critics argue that Newsom's policies encourage the chemical castration of healthy boys and the removal of healthy breasts from young girls, procedures that many consider mutilation rather than care. While Newsom presents these policies as necessary steps toward inclusivity and equality, they raise serious ethical, medical, and social concerns that cannot be ignored. As California continues to lead the charge in transgender rights, the nation must carefully consider whether Newsom's approach is truly in the best interests of vulnerable populations or whether it is part of a larger agenda that risks irreversible harm in the name of progress.

Support for Transgender Students: The Impact of Newsom's Policies

Governor Gavin Newsom's ardent support for transgender rights has included a strong push for policies that allow transgender students in California to participate in school sports and use facilities that align with their gender identity. His advocacy for these issues, particularly his endorsement of the California Interscholastic Federation's (CIF) policy in 2021, which permits transgender students to compete in sports according to their gender identity, has been hailed as a victory for equality and inclusion by some. However, from a conservative standpoint, these policies are deeply troubling, as they raise serious concerns about fairness, safety, and the erosion of traditional norms in education and sports.

While Newsom's support for transgender students is framed as a progressive step toward inclusivity and human rights, the reality is that these policies can have serious negative consequences, particularly for biological women. When Newsom praises the CIF's decision as a "step forward" for equality, he overlooks the long-term effects these policies have on female athletes, who may now be forced to compete against biologically male competitors in sports that require physical strength, endurance, and skill. The fundamental question at the heart of this issue is: Should biological sex or gender identity determine eligibility in sports and access to facilities?

The CIF Policy: Unfair to Female Athletes

In 2021, Newsom expressed his full support for the California Interscholastic Federation (CIF) policy, which allows transgender students to compete in high school sports consistent with their gender identity, regardless of their biological sex. This decision was portrayed as an important step in ensuring that transgender students have equal opportunities in school sports. However, from a conservative perspective, this policy undermines the integrity of women's sports and creates an unlevel playing field.

The core issue here is the biological advantage that transgender women (biological males who identify as female) often have when competing against biological women. Sports such as track and field, swimming, and wrestling require physical strength, speed, and endurance—attributes where biological males, even after transitioning, often have a natural advantage due to factors like muscle mass, bone density, and cardiovascular capacity. In many cases, transgender women have been able to dominate in women's sports, defeating female athletes who have trained for years in their respective disciplines.

For example, in Connecticut, several transgender athletes, who were biologically male, began competing in women's high school track events, leading to controversial victories in state championships and sparking a legal battle. Female athletes who had trained their entire lives to win titles and earn college scholarships were left at a disadvantage, and many felt that their hard work was rendered meaningless by policies that allowed transgender women to compete on the same playing field. This issue is not limited to Connecticut; similar instances have occurred across the country, and the debate is intensifying as more states, including California, adopt similar policies.

From a conservative standpoint, allowing transgender athletes to compete in women's sports not only diminishes the hard-won opportunities for female athletes but also creates a dangerous precedent for the future of competitive sports. Female athletes are often fighting for the same opportunities, funding, and recognition as their male counterparts, and policies like Newsom's threaten to undermine progress that has been made in achieving gender equity in athletics.

The Safety Concerns: Changing Rooms and Bathrooms

Newsom's policies also extend to the use of school facilities, including bathrooms and locker rooms, where students are allowed to use the facilities that correspond with their gender identity. While this is framed as a measure of respect and inclusion for transgender students, it raises significant concerns about the privacy and safety of other students, particularly young girls. Many parents, teachers, and students are uncomfortable with the idea of biological males being permitted to access facilities designated for women, and they argue that it exposes girls and women to potential harm and invasion of privacy.

Allowing biological males who identify as female to use women's bathrooms, locker rooms, and changing facilities presents the risk of exposure and assault, especially in situations where girls are undressing or in vulnerable positions. While Newsom and his supporters argue that transgender individuals are at a higher risk of violence and discrimination, the reality is that allowing males in female-designated spaces can increase the potential for misconduct. Critics argue that this undermines the safety and privacy of female students who should be able to expect a certain level of security when using school facilities.

In California, Newsom's support for these policies has been contentious, with many parents, especially those with young daughters, voicing concerns about the lack of safeguards. While transgender rights advocates argue that the fear of harassment is exaggerated, the reality remains that some girls feel uncomfortable sharing locker rooms or changing areas with individuals who are biologically male. The issue of access to facilities that align with gender identity is complex, but many Californians believe that biological sex, not gender identity, should determine access to such spaces in order to maintain the integrity of women's privacy and safety.

The Psychological Impact on Minors

Another area where Newsom's policies have drawn criticism is in regard to the psychological and emotional impact of encouraging minors to explore their gender identity through policies that allow them to change sports teams and access facilities based on gender identity. Some mental health professionals have raised concerns that, in an environment that is increasingly affirming of transgender identity, young people might make decisions that are driven by societal pressure rather than a thorough understanding of their own identity.

While Newsom's policies are framed as a means of reducing stigma and ensuring equal rights for transgender youth, critics argue that these measures might inadvertently reinforce gender confusion among minors who are still undergoing emotional and psychological development. Many minors experience gender dysphoria at different stages of their adolescence, and some grow out of it as they mature. By encouraging children to act on their gender confusion without appropriate psychological counseling or exploration, these policies may actually compound the issue in the long run.

Some Californians point out that there are no easy answers when it comes to helping children navigate gender identity issues, and that medical treatments or transitions might not be the right solution for every child. Rather than pushing gender-affirming policies that encourage young people to make permanent decisions about their identity, some argue that society should focus on offering more psychological support and mental health services to help children navigate their feelings without rushing them into medical or social transitions.

The Backlash Against Newsom's Policies

As Newsom's support for transgender students continues to be a key issue in California, backlash is growing both within the state and beyond. Many conservative groups, parents, and even some liberal individuals are concerned that Newsom's policies are too far-reaching, particularly in a state as influential as California. The debate over transgender rights in schools has become one of the most contentious issues in recent years, with many fearing that these policies prioritize the rights of a small minority over the rights and safety of the majority.

Newsom's support for policies that allow transgender students to participate in sports and use school facilities according to their gender identity is framed as an effort to promote inclusion and protect vulnerable individuals. However, as the controversies surrounding these policies continue to escalate, it is clear that there are significant concerns about the fairness, safety, and long-term implications of such measures. Critics argue that while the intention may be to protect transgender individuals, the practical consequences can be damaging to others, particularly women and children, who may feel marginalized or unsafe as a result.

The Broader Implications of Newsom's Policies

The issue of transgender students in California is part of a larger, national debate about the role of government in regulating gender identity in schools. As California leads the way in implementing these policies, other states are closely watching and assessing the potential consequences of such measures. Newsom's aggressive push for transgender rights in schools sets a dangerous precedent for the future of education and sports across the country, one that may have far-reaching effects on students, parents, and educators who are already grappling with the complexities of gender identity in the classroom.

From a conservative standpoint, Newsom's policies are an overreach of government authority that puts the needs and safety of the majority at risk in favor of promoting a progressive agenda. Many Californians argue that the biological differences between males and females should be recognized in schools and that policies regarding sports and facilities should prioritize fairness, privacy, and safety. The ongoing legal battles, protests, and public debates surrounding Newsom's policies reflect the growing concern that policies which favor one group at the expense of another can undermine social cohesion and create unnecessary divisions.

Gavin Newsom's support for transgender students in California has undoubtedly advanced the cause of transgender rights. However, from a conservative perspective, his policies create significant challenges for the safety, fairness, and well-being of other students, particularly biological females. Allowing transgender students to participate in sports and access school facilities according to their gender identity may be seen as a step forward for equality, but it also raises critical questions about the impact on the integrity of women's sports, the privacy and safety of female students, and the potential for long-term psychological harm to minors who are not fully equipped to make decisions about their gender identity. As California continues to push forward with these policies, it is essential that the broader implications are considered, not only for transgender students but for all students who may be affected by these changes.

Governor Gavin Newsom's stance on transgender issues has led California to become a focal point in the broader national conversation on gender identity, particularly concerning the rights and treatment of transgender individuals. While Newsom's policies, such as allowing transgender individuals to participate in sports consistent with their gender identity and access facilities based on gender identity, are often hailed as progressive victories, they also present significant challenges and consequences.

From a conservative perspective, Newsom's policies raise serious concerns about fairness, safety, and the potential long-term harm caused to vulnerable populations, particularly women and children. Allowing transgender women, A.K.A. men, to compete in women's sports undermines the integrity of women's athletics, creating a situation where females are at an unfair disadvantage. Additionally, the expansion of transgender rights in school facilities, including bathrooms and locker rooms, has created uncomfortable and unsafe conditions for many students, particularly young girls who may be forced to share these spaces with individuals who retain male anatomy.

Newsom's support for gender-affirming healthcare for minors, including puberty blockers and hormone therapy, further complicates the picture. While these treatments are presented as necessary for the well-being of transgender youth, the decision to administer such powerful medical interventions to minors raises ethical questions. The irreversible nature of some of these procedures and the potential for long-term physical and psychological consequences should not be overlooked. The tension between supporting the rights of transgender individuals and protecting the well-being of vulnerable minors is at the heart of this debate, and Newsom's policies fail to strike a balance that adequately addresses the risks involved.

California's approach to transgender rights, as championed by Newsom, is part of a broader cultural shift that seeks to normalize transgender identity and treatment, but this shift comes at a cost. From the disruption of women's sports to the potential risks posed to children through medical treatments, Newsom's policies have ignited a significant conversation about the direction of public policy on gender identity. While the desire to ensure dignity and safety for transgender individuals is laudable, it must not come at the expense of fairness, safety, and the protection of other individuals' rights.

As the conversation on transgenderism continues to evolve, it is essential that policymakers like Newsom consider the broader societal impacts of their decisions and ensure that the rights of all individuals—regardless of gender identity—are respected and protected. The policies implemented under Newsom's leadership have opened the door for important discussions on equality, inclusion, and human rights, but they also highlight the need for greater caution and deliberation when enacting laws that affect the lives and safety of so many people. The real challenge moving forward will be to find a balance that respects the rights of transgender individuals while also protecting the safety, fairness, and well-being of everyone in society.

Chapter 5

The Future of California

Under Governor Gavin Newsom's leadership, California has become a laboratory for progressive policies, which have left an indelible mark on the state's economy. Newsom has championed initiatives to expand healthcare access, increase taxes on the wealthy, and drive investments in green energy. While these policies were designed to promote equity and sustainability, they have also sparked significant economic challenges and debates about their effectiveness.

One of Newsom's most significant policy initiatives has been his focus on expanding healthcare access. In 2020, Newsom extended Medi-Cal, California's Medicaid program, to include undocumented adults aged 26 to 49. As a result, approximately 1.1 million additional people gained healthcare coverage, costing the state billions. By 2024, the state budget allocated more than $20 billion annually to Medi-Cal, making up over 20% of California's total budget. While proponents argue that universal healthcare is a moral imperative and a long-term investment in public health, critics point out that such a massive outlay of taxpayer money comes at a cost to other sectors of the economy. The state has also struggled with growing healthcare costs, and there are concerns that the increasing demand for services may outpace the state's ability to provide them without further tax increases or cuts to other services.

Newsom's progressive economic policies also include efforts to increase taxes on high earners and corporations. Under his leadership, California implemented one of the highest state income tax rates in the nation, reaching 13.3% for individuals earning over $1 million. This was part of a broader strategy to fund public services like education, housing, and healthcare. In 2020, the state's top 1% of earners paid 49.2% of all state income taxes. However, the state's aggressive taxation policies have drawn criticism from business leaders and conservatives, who argue that the high taxes burden businesses and discourage investment. California has seen an outflow of high-income residents, and research by the Hoover Institution found that between 2007 and 2017, California lost nearly 1 million residents to other states, particularly Texas and Florida, both of which have no state income tax.

Despite these taxes, the state's economic growth has been constrained by what many see as an overreliance on industries like technology and entertainment, which are highly volatile. When economic downturns hit, such as the 2020 pandemic-related recession, California's heavy reliance on a small number of wealthy taxpayers made it vulnerable to sudden revenue shortfalls.

Additionally, Newsom's push for green energy has been ambitious, with a target to achieve 100% carbon-free electricity by 2045. While California's green energy sector has grown, the transition has come at a steep cost. California has spent billions on renewable energy programs and subsidies, with some estimates placing total state spending on clean energy and climate programs at over $20 billion. Critics argue that Newsom's policies have failed to sufficiently address the challenges of maintaining grid reliability. In 2020, California experienced rolling blackouts during a heatwave, which some critics blamed on the state's increasing reliance on renewable energy without sufficient backup capacity from natural gas plants. While Newsom's administration has pushed for clean energy as a long-term economic benefit, the immediate costs—both in terms of financial investment and reliability—have caused significant concern.

Tech Industry and Job Creation

California has long been home to Silicon Valley, the global epicenter of the tech industry. Under Newsom's leadership, the tech sector has remained a driving force in the state's economy, contributing to approximately 10% of the state's GDP. However, Newsom's policies have been met with mixed reactions from business leaders, particularly as the state has become increasingly expensive for both businesses and workers.

Newsom has made efforts to foster job growth in California, particularly in the tech and green energy sectors. He has allocated funding to expand broadband access in underserved areas, invested in workforce development programs, and promoted STEM education initiatives. For instance, Newsom's administration launched the California for All initiative in 2020, designed to attract talent to the state and address the tech industry's diversity gaps. His efforts to attract companies like Tesla, which has moved its headquarters to Texas, have been met with some success, but the overall impact on job creation has been uneven.

While Newsom's policies have helped foster innovation in sectors like tech and green energy, his administration's handling of business regulations has raised concerns. California has some of the strictest regulations for businesses, particularly around employment law. The California Consumer Privacy Act (CCPA), signed by Newsom in 2018, is one of the strictest data privacy laws in the nation. While many argue that such regulations are necessary for consumer protection, they have placed a significant burden on businesses, particularly startups and small enterprises that struggle to meet compliance costs. As a result, some tech companies have opted to relocate or expand outside of California, where regulatory environments are more business-friendly.

Newsom's handling of the state's housing crisis has also hurt the tech industry, as rising housing costs and an ongoing shortage of affordable homes have made it difficult for tech workers to live near their workplaces. San Francisco, once considered the heart of the tech industry, has seen a significant outflow of tech talent due to skyrocketing rents. According to a 2022 survey, over 60% of tech workers said they were considering leaving the Bay Area due to high living costs. Despite Newsom's promises to tackle housing affordability, the state's housing market has only become more strained under his leadership. The state's housing deficit has reached over 3.5 million units, and housing prices in cities like San Francisco and Los Angeles have soared, exacerbating economic inequality and reducing access to talent in the state's key industries.

Housing Affordability and Economic Inequality

One of the most pressing issues during Newsom's governorship has been California's persistent housing crisis, which has worsened despite numerous attempts to address it. California has long had one of the most expensive housing markets in the nation, and under Newsom's leadership, the problem has only intensified. Home prices in California have more than doubled since 2010, with the median price of a single-family home reaching $800,000 in 2022—nearly three times the national median. The crisis has created a severe affordability gap, where many residents, particularly in urban areas, are priced out of homeownership.

In 2020, Newsom set a goal of building 3.5 million new homes by 2025 to help address the shortage. However, this ambitious target has largely gone unmet. By 2023, California had built only 1.2 million new homes, far short of the goal. Newsom has tried to address the issue by streamlining regulations and promoting zoning reforms, but these efforts have been met with resistance from local governments and communities. Many cities and towns are reluctant to approve higher-density housing projects due to concerns about traffic, local infrastructure, and changes to community character. As a result, Newsom's policies have not had the desired effect on reducing the housing affordability gap, leaving many low- and middle-income Californians struggling to find affordable housing.

The crisis has also contributed to rising income inequality. California has the highest poverty rate in the country, with more than 13% of residents living below the federal poverty line. However, when accounting for housing costs, this figure rises to 19%. In California, the wealthiest 1% of households earn more than 25% of all income, while the bottom 50% take home just 15%. Newsom's progressive tax policies have exacerbated this divide, with high-income earners paying the majority of state taxes. While this approach is intended to fund social services and reduce inequality, it has also made California increasingly reliant on a small group of wealthy individuals, making the state vulnerable to economic downturns. The state's wealth gap continues to grow, as tech workers, executives, and entrepreneurs enjoy substantial earnings while millions of others face stagnant wages and unaffordable living costs.

Moreover, Newsom's push for green energy has not provided the promised relief to the state's housing or economic inequality issues. While policies promoting renewable energy have created jobs in the clean energy sector, the transition has come at a significant cost to businesses and consumers. As of 2022, California had spent over $50 billion on renewable energy and related projects, yet energy prices have risen significantly. California residents pay some of the highest electricity rates in the nation, which disproportionately impacts low-income households, further contributing to economic inequality.

Governor Gavin Newsom's economic policies, while well-intentioned, have faced significant challenges in addressing

California's most pressing issues: the housing crisis, economic inequality, and business growth. His ambitious plans to expand healthcare, increase taxes on the wealthy, and push for green energy have all had mixed results, contributing to both the state's economic growth and its growing burdens. As California continues to grapple with these issues, it is crucial to consider how Newsom's policies will affect not just the state's future but also the quality of life for its residents. For voters looking ahead to 2028, it's clear that the economic path Newsom has charted will have far-reaching consequences for California's competitiveness, affordability, and ability to provide for its most vulnerable citizens.

Social Change: Equality, Health, and Education

Governor Gavin Newsom's healthcare reforms have been central to his progressive agenda, with a focus on expanding access to care, reducing costs, and addressing health disparities. His administration has introduced several initiatives aimed at making healthcare more accessible and affordable, but the effects have been mixed, with both successes and challenges.

One of Newsom's most significant moves in healthcare reform was the expansion of Medi-Cal, California's Medicaid program. In 2020, Newsom extended Medi-Cal eligibility to include undocumented residents aged 26 to 49. This expansion allowed approximately 1.1 million additional individuals to access healthcare coverage, a move that garnered both praise for its inclusivity and concern over its long-term costs. By 2024, California had allocated more than $20 billion annually for Medi-Cal, making up over 20% of the state's total budget. While the expansion is considered a win for public health, critics argue that the rising costs associated with such expansive coverage could eventually lead to cuts in other essential services, such as education or public safety, or require increased taxes to maintain the program's sustainability.

In addition to Medi-Cal, Newsom launched the CalRx program, aimed at reducing prescription drug prices. This initiative allows the state to negotiate directly with drug manufacturers to offer lower-cost prescription medications to residents. In 2021, California reached a deal with Amgen to lower the price of epinephrine for allergy sufferers by more than 50%, a victory for Newsom's administration. However, despite these efforts, prescription drug prices in California remain some of the highest in the nation, and the effectiveness of CalRx has been questioned by many healthcare experts. Critics argue that Newsom's efforts do not go far enough to address the systemic issues in the pharmaceutical industry, such as price gouging, monopolistic practices, and a lack of competition.

Newsom also introduced other healthcare reforms aimed at improving mental health services, particularly in response to the growing homelessness crisis. In 2020, he announced $750 million in funding for homelessness prevention and mental health services, but many have argued that this money has been poorly allocated. Despite these efforts, the state continues to face significant challenges in providing adequate care for its most vulnerable populations. California's mental health crisis remains one of the most pressing public health issues, and Newsom's failure to address it in a meaningful way has drawn widespread criticism.

Education

Newsom's policies on education have focused on increasing funding, improving access to quality schooling, and addressing disparities in educational opportunities. In his first year as governor, Newsom allocated $15 billion to improve K-12 education, including an increase in funding for schools serving disadvantaged students. However, the state's public education system remains one of the most underfunded in the nation, with California spending just $12,000 per student annually, far below the national average of $13,000. The gap in funding is especially significant in lower-income districts, where students often lack access to the resources needed for success, such as updated textbooks, technology, and extracurricular programs.

Despite Newsom's promises to address these disparities, educational outcomes for California's low-income and minority students remain poor. According to a 2019 study by the Public Policy Institute of California, students in lower-income districts are twice as likely to drop out of school as those in wealthier areas. While Newsom has made some strides in increasing funding for disadvantaged schools, critics argue that his efforts have not gone far enough to address the root causes of inequality in California's public education system, including overcrowded classrooms, underpaid teachers, and a lack of resources in low-income areas.

On higher education, Newsom has pushed for increased funding for public universities and community colleges. His 2020 budget included a $1.5 billion increase in funding for California's public universities, part of a broader effort to make higher education more affordable and accessible. However, tuition at the University of California and California State University systems has continued to rise, making it increasingly difficult for students from low-income backgrounds to afford college. While Newsom has made efforts to support community colleges and make vocational training more accessible, California's higher education system remains one of the most expensive in the country, creating barriers to educational attainment for many residents.

Criminal Justice and Equality

Governor Newsom has been a strong proponent of criminal justice reform, advocating for measures aimed at reducing incarceration rates, addressing systemic inequality, and reforming the state's criminal justice system. One of his first acts as governor was to halt the death penalty in California, a move that was met with both praise from advocates for justice reform and backlash from opponents of abolition. The moratorium, which effectively placed a halt on executions, was a symbolic step toward reforming California's criminal justice system, and Newsom's administration has continued to push for changes to reduce the prison population and address racial disparities.

Newsom has also supported efforts to reduce sentences for non-violent offenders, particularly those convicted of drug-related crimes. In 2020, he signed SB 1006, a bill that expanded eligibility for parole for individuals convicted of drug offenses. This bill was part of Newsom's broader effort to reduce the state's prison population, which has historically been one of the largest in the nation. While Newsom's efforts to reduce incarceration have been praised by criminal justice reform advocates, critics argue that the reduction in sentences does not go far enough to address the root causes of criminal behavior, such as poverty, mental illness, and lack of education, nor does it sufficiently focus on rehabilitation programs for inmates.

In response to the Black Lives Matter movement and growing calls for racial justice, Newsom has made efforts to address systemic inequality within California's criminal justice system. His administration has introduced $300 million in funding to support police reform initiatives and provide training on racial bias and de-escalation tactics. While some progress has been made, including the reduction in police violence and investigations into police misconduct, California continues to face significant challenges in addressing racial disparities within the criminal justice system. In 2021, a report from the California Department of Justice revealed that Black Californians were still three times more likely to be arrested than white Californians, despite making up only 6% of the state's population.

Critics argue that Newsom's reforms, while well-intentioned, have not done enough to reduce the disproportionate impact of the criminal justice system on communities of color. They argue that his policies have focused too much on reducing sentences and not enough on addressing the systemic factors that contribute to racial disparities in policing and sentencing. While Newsom has made strides toward criminal justice reform, many believe his efforts have been insufficient to bring about the structural changes needed to achieve true racial equity in California.

Governor Gavin Newsom's approach to healthcare, education, and criminal justice reform has been marked by ambitious progressive policies aimed at reducing inequality and improving access to essential services. However, the effectiveness of these policies has been a subject of debate, with critics pointing to rising costs, insufficient resources, and a lack of meaningful progress in addressing disparities. As California continues to grapple with these challenges, it is crucial to consider how Newsom's social policies have impacted both the state's residents and the long-term sustainability of its public systems. Voters, particularly those considering him for national office in 2028, will need to weigh the outcomes of these reforms, as well as the challenges that remain, in determining whether his leadership has truly delivered on the promises of equality and social change.

Environmental Policies

Governor Gavin Newsom has made environmental sustainability a cornerstone of his leadership, with ambitious goals aimed at making California a leader in green energy and climate action. One of the most prominent elements of his environmental agenda is the state's commitment to achieving 100% renewable energy by 2045, a goal enshrined in the California Clean Energy and Pollution Reduction Act of 2015, which Newsom has continued to champion. The transition to renewable energy is part of the state's broader efforts to combat climate change, reduce greenhouse gas emissions, and promote sustainability. However, the ambitious timeline raises questions about the feasibility of such goals and the potential costs associated with them.

As of 2023, California generates about 36% of its electricity from renewable sources, including solar, wind, and hydroelectric power, with solar power leading the charge. The state has aggressively incentivized the adoption of solar panels and wind turbines, and California is home to some of the largest solar farms in the world. However, achieving 100% renewable energy by 2045 presents significant challenges, including the intermittent nature of solar and wind energy. These sources require substantial investment in energy storage technology, such as batteries, to ensure a stable power supply during periods of high demand or low generation. Despite California's leadership in renewable energy, the state still faces significant reliability issues in its grid, as evidenced by the rolling blackouts that occurred during the summer of 2020. These blackouts were partially attributed to the state's heavy reliance on renewable energy sources without sufficient backup from natural gas or other forms of stable power generation.

In response to these challenges, Newsom has promoted initiatives like the California Energy Storage Roadmap, which aims to significantly increase energy storage capacity to support renewable energy generation. However, critics argue that while these efforts are promising, the necessary investments in infrastructure are far behind what is needed to make the grid fully reliable. The state has also spent billions of dollars on renewable energy incentives and subsidies, but some argue that these investments have not yielded sufficient returns, especially considering the ongoing energy crises and price volatility in the state's energy market. Moreover, Newsom's administration has been criticized for a lack of a clear, cohesive strategy for transitioning away from fossil fuels while also ensuring economic stability and energy affordability for residents.

The push for electric vehicles (EVs) has also been a key element of Newsom's climate agenda. In 2020, Newsom signed an executive order that mandates the sale of all new passenger cars in California to be zero-emission vehicles by 2035. While the state has led the nation in EV adoption, with over 500,000 electric vehicles on the road in 2020, critics point out that Newsom's goals may not be feasible without addressing key infrastructure gaps. The state's charging network, for example, remains underdeveloped in many areas, especially in rural regions where residents have fewer resources and options to make the switch to EVs. Furthermore, the transition to EVs requires significant investment in charging infrastructure and energy grid upgrades. Although California has allocated $10 billion to expand the EV market, the transition is complicated by the high upfront costs of EVs, even with state subsidies, which continue to be out of reach for many low- and middle-income residents.

While Newsom's green energy policies have positioned California as a leader in renewable energy, the state's ambitious climate targets have yet to be fully realized, and the costs and practical implications of achieving these goals remain contentious. The state's ongoing energy struggles, rising costs for consumers, and uneven access to clean energy alternatives raise questions about the broader impact of Newsom's green energy push on both the state's residents and its economy.

Wildfire Prevention and Environmental Protection

California's wildfire crisis has been an ongoing challenge, one that has worsened under Newsom's leadership despite his administration's focus on environmental protection. The state is experiencing an increasing frequency and intensity of wildfires, driven in part by climate change, a growing population in fire-prone areas, and the state's failure to implement effective wildfire prevention strategies. In 2020 alone, California experienced 9,639 wildfires that scorched more than 4.3 million acres of land, making it the largest wildfire season on record. The 2020 wildfires also destroyed more than 10,000 homes and caused over $10 billion in damages. Newsom declared a state of emergency in response to the fires and requested federal assistance to combat the blazes, but critics argue that his administration's response to the crisis was insufficient.

One of Newsom's key wildfire prevention initiatives has been the Forest Management Task Force, which he created in 2019 to address the growing threat of wildfires by improving forest management practices, including controlled burns, clearing brush, and thinning dense forests. The state has allocated hundreds of millions of dollars to fund these efforts, but the impact has been limited. Critics argue that California's forest management practices have been inconsistent, and in some areas, the state's reliance on controlled burns has been poorly executed, leading to unintended consequences. For instance, in 2020, a controlled burn in the Angeles National Forest led to a large wildfire that spread out of control. Despite Newsom's efforts to streamline and improve forest management practices, wildfires continue to rage with increasing intensity.

In addition to forest management, Newsom has pushed for climate change mitigation measures that he argues will reduce the long-term risks associated with wildfires. These measures include California's commitment to carbon neutrality by 2045, the expansion of renewable energy sources, and the phasing out of fossil fuels. However, environmental experts warn that climate change is making California's wildfire season longer and more severe, and Newsom's policies have not adequately addressed the underlying issues that contribute to the worsening crisis. Despite billions of dollars spent on wildfire response and prevention, many regions still lack the infrastructure and resources to combat wildfires effectively, and communities are left vulnerable.

The state has also faced criticism for its wildfire response systems, which many argue are underfunded and ill-prepared to handle the scale of modern wildfires. During the 2020 wildfire season, thousands of first responders were stretched thin, and resources such as helicopters, fire engines, and personnel were insufficient to handle the unprecedented number of fires. Newsom's administration was forced to call in federal and out-of-state resources to combat the fires, highlighting the state's reliance on federal support rather than its own capabilities. While Newsom has made efforts to improve preparedness, the ongoing wildfire crisis suggests that his administration's policies have not been fully effective in mitigating the damage caused by wildfires.

Water Crisis and Infrastructure

California's water crisis has been a persistent issue that has only grown worse under Newsom's leadership, with droughts, population growth, and climate change placing immense pressure on the state's water resources. California has faced record droughts in recent years, with 2021 marking the third-driest year on record since 1895. The state is highly dependent on snowpack and rainfall for its water supply, and when both are insufficient, water shortages exacerbate the challenges faced by residents, farmers, and businesses.

Newsom's response to the water crisis has included a focus on water conservation measures and water infrastructure upgrades.

In 2020, Newsom signed an executive order aimed at cutting California's urban water use by 20% and investing in water recycling and desalination technologies. The state has committed $5 billion to improve water management, increase efficiency, and provide water to communities in need. However, critics argue that Newsom's initiatives are not enough to address the long-term sustainability of California's water supply. In 2021, 71% of California's water use still went to agriculture, raising concerns about the sustainability of irrigation practices in the face of growing demand.

Additionally, Newsom's administration has faced criticism for its handling of the State Water Project, which supplies water to over 27 million people. Infrastructure issues, such as aging dams and pipes, and disputes over water allocation have hampered efforts to ensure a reliable and equitable water supply. Some have argued that Newsom's policies have been too focused on short-term solutions, rather than addressing the systemic challenges facing the state's water infrastructure. The California WaterFix, a controversial plan to modernize the state's water infrastructure, has faced delays, funding shortfalls, and legal challenges, leaving the state without a clear path forward to ensure long-term water security.

In response to increasing water scarcity, Newsom has also promoted water conservation measures, including restrictions on outdoor water use, restrictions on water-intensive crops, and mandatory water cuts for cities facing shortages. However, critics argue that these measures disproportionately affect low-income communities, farmers, and rural areas that rely on water-intensive industries like agriculture.

Governor Gavin Newsom's environmental policies reflect his commitment to addressing climate change and promoting sustainability in California. However, the challenges faced by the state—ranging from energy grid reliability and wildfire destruction to water scarcity—highlight the complexity of achieving ambitious environmental goals while managing the economic and logistical realities of a state as large and diverse as California. Newsom's aggressive pursuit of green energy, wildfire prevention, and climate change mitigation has had varying degrees of success, but the broader impacts on residents, businesses, and infrastructure raise important questions about the long-term feasibility of these policies. As voters look ahead to 2028, Newsom's environmental legacy will be a key factor in evaluating his readiness to lead the nation through one of the most pressing crises of our time.

California's Role in National Politics

Governor Gavin Newsom, with his ambitious political agenda and progressive policies, has positioned himself as a potential frontrunner for the 2028 Democratic presidential nomination. As the governor of California, the nation's most populous state, Newsom has a platform that has allowed him to implement sweeping policies on issues ranging from healthcare to climate change, making him an attractive candidate for the progressive wing of the Democratic Party. His ability to navigate California's diverse political landscape—balancing the needs of urban and rural areas, different socioeconomic groups, and an increasingly polarized electorate—has been a key component of his leadership style.

Newsom's appeal as a national leader lies in his strong ties to the progressive base of the Democratic Party. His support for universal healthcare, evidenced by his expansion of Medi-Cal and his advocacy for single-payer healthcare in California, has made him a champion for left-leaning voters who seek comprehensive, government-funded healthcare. Similarly, his bold environmental initiatives, such as the state's goal of achieving 100% clean energy by 2045 and his push for widespread adoption of electric vehicles, align with the priorities of climate-conscious progressives. Newsom's policies on gender equality, racial justice, and criminal justice reform, including his efforts to reduce sentences for nonviolent offenders and his opposition to the death penalty, have made him a strong advocate for social justice.

In addition to his policy stances, Newsom's personal charisma and communication style play a significant role in his appeal. He is known for his eloquence and confidence, often portraying himself as a pragmatic, yet bold, progressive leader. Newsom's ability to speak directly to the challenges of working-class Americans, particularly those in urban centers, has allowed him to build a reputation as a leader who understands the struggles of everyday people while pushing for systemic change. His rhetorical style is polished, frequently deploying a combination of empathy and intellectual rigor that resonates with a variety of Democratic constituencies.

However, Newsom's political rise has not been without its challenges. Despite his strong record on certain progressive issues, he has also faced significant criticism, particularly in his handling of California's most pressing issues—wildfires, housing affordability, and the state's homelessness crisis. These ongoing problems could undermine his ability to appeal to a broader electorate, especially in swing states where issues like housing and homelessness are less pronounced. While Newsom may be seen as a hero among progressives, his ability to bridge the divide between the left and the moderates in the Democratic Party remains uncertain.

As a national candidate, Newsom's California-centric policies may be both a strength and a liability. His record of progressive accomplishments in one of the most liberal states in the country has earned him respect among his base, but it may also present a challenge when trying to gain support in battleground states where voters may be skeptical of California's high taxes, business regulations, and progressive social policies. His push for clean energy and taxing the wealthy, while popular among progressives, could alienate moderate and conservative voters in swing states like Michigan, Florida, or Ohio—states that are crucial for any Democratic presidential candidate to win in 2028.

Political Challenges and Controversies

Despite his promising political trajectory, Newsom's past controversies pose significant challenges to his potential presidential run. His personal scandals, including his affair with his former campaign manager's wife and the French Laundry incident, which occurred during California's COVID-19 lockdown, have raised questions about his judgment and character. The French Laundry scandal, in particular, was a significant public relations disaster. Newsom was photographed dining indoors at a lavish Napa Valley restaurant in November 2020, violating his own stay-at-home orders. This incident, perceived as a blatant example of hypocrisy, fueled criticism from both Republicans and moderates, as well as some progressives who felt Newsom was not leading by example. The scandal made headlines across the country and became a focal point for his opponents, undermining his credibility as a leader who could navigate a national crisis with integrity.

In addition to personal controversies, Newsom has faced challenges related to his leadership style. While he is often praised for his eloquence and confidence, some critics argue that he is more style than substance. His handling of California's housing crisis, wildfires, and homelessness epidemic has drawn widespread scrutiny. Despite his ambitious goals for addressing these issues, Newsom's tenure has seen little concrete progress, especially in the area of affordable housing, where the state's housing market continues to be one of the most expensive in the nation. As California grapples with an estimated 3.5 million-unit housing deficit, Newsom's inability to effectively address this issue could be used against him in a national campaign.

Furthermore, Newsom's record on criminal justice reform and police accountability could also be a double-edged sword in a national race. His efforts to reduce the prison population, eliminate the death penalty, and decriminalize certain offenses have been popular among progressives. However, these policies have made him a target for conservatives, who argue that they are too lenient and contribute to rising crime rates in urban areas. In 2020, Newsom's approval ratings dipped significantly, partly due to frustrations over his handling of California's crime wave, which included a rise in car burglaries, drug overdoses, and violent crimes in major cities like Los Angeles and San Francisco. While Newsom has attempted to tackle criminal justice reform in a manner consistent with his progressive values, his record could be weaponized by opponents who paint him as soft on crime.

These personal scandals and leadership challenges are not just minor distractions; they have the potential to affect Newsom's ability to mount a successful presidential campaign. His controversies could fuel negative perceptions of him among moderate voters and swing-state Democrats, which could severely limit his chances in a general election.

California as a Political Model

Another key question surrounding Newsom's potential 2028 run is whether the political model he has implemented in California can be replicated on a national level. California, under Newsom's leadership, has become a laboratory for progressive policy, from ambitious climate change goals to universal healthcare expansion and criminal justice reform. However, many of these policies—while popular in California—face considerable challenges when considered for broader application on a national scale.

California's tax structure, which includes some of the highest income and sales taxes in the nation, could be a tough sell to voters in states with lower tax burdens. As a state that levies a top income tax rate of 13.3% for individuals earning over $1 million, California has driven away many wealthy residents and businesses to states with no income tax, such as Texas and Florida. These states are not only cheaper to live in, but they also have less stringent regulations, which appeal to business owners, entrepreneurs, and professionals. A national policy that mirrors California's high-tax, high-regulation model could face significant opposition, especially in battleground states where lower taxes and deregulation are seen as keys to economic growth.

Similarly, Newsom's climate change policies—while groundbreaking and important for California—might not resonate with voters in other parts of the country. California's push for 100% clean energy by 2045 and its aggressive targets for electric vehicles could be difficult to implement in states that rely on fossil fuels, such as West Virginia or Texas. National efforts to phase out gas-powered vehicles, for instance, would face significant resistance from the automotive and oil industries, both of which are major sources of jobs and revenue in several states. The cost of transitioning to renewable energy and the regulatory burden it places on businesses could alienate key constituencies in states where jobs in the oil and gas industry are a major part of the economy.

Another challenge to Newsom's political model is California's housing crisis. Despite significant efforts to build affordable housing, California continues to have one of the highest rates of homelessness in the nation. With over 180,000 homeless individuals living in the state, Newsom's inability to solve the housing crisis could be a liability on the national stage. If Newsom were to advocate for similar policies in other states, including increased housing regulations and government interventions, he would need to address the concerns of voters in states where the housing market is more affordable and less regulated.

Moreover, Newsom's progressive social policies—including efforts to expand access to healthcare for undocumented residents and his support for criminal justice reforms—have positioned him as a progressive champion in California. However, these same policies could present challenges in more conservative states, where immigration, healthcare reform, and policing remain contentious issues. Newsom's stance on immigration reform and his support for sanctuary cities and sanctuary state policies may alienate voters who prioritize stricter border controls and more conservative approaches to immigration.

The central question for voters, then, is whether Newsom's experience in California can be effectively translated to the national stage. While Newsom's progressive record and national ambitions align with the Democratic Party's growing shift to the left, the unique political climate of California may not be replicable in other states, particularly in swing states that are critical for any Democratic presidential candidate.

Gavin Newsom's potential 2028 presidential campaign will undoubtedly center around his progressive policies and leadership record in California. His appeal to progressive voters and his policy accomplishments in healthcare, climate change, and criminal justice reform position him as a formidable candidate within his party. However, his personal scandals, leadership challenges, and the limitations of California's political model raise important questions about his ability to appeal to a broader electorate. Whether Newsom's vision for California can be successfully exported to the national stage remains to be seen. As voters weigh his candidacy, they will need to consider both his accomplishments and his controversies, as well as the broader implications of applying California's progressive model to the nation as a whole.

Public Perception and Legacy

Governor Gavin Newsom's leadership has been a subject of both admiration and criticism throughout his tenure in California. His public approval ratings have fluctuated significantly, reflecting the mixed responses to his progressive policies, handling of crises, and the ongoing controversies that have followed him throughout his career. As of early 2024, Newsom's approval rating in California was around 50%, with higher ratings among younger voters, urban residents, and progressives, while his disapproval was notably higher among conservatives, rural communities, and small business owners.

Newsom's approval was at its highest early in his governorship, particularly in 2019, when he took office with ambitious promises of progressive reforms in healthcare, housing, and the environment. His leadership during the initial stages of the COVID-19 pandemic also garnered praise for his decisive actions, including statewide lockdowns, mask mandates, and a push for widespread testing. Newsom's bold approach during the pandemic initially led to high approval ratings, as many Californians supported the aggressive stance to protect public health.

However, as the pandemic wore on, his approval began to wane. By mid-2020, Newsom's French Laundry scandal—where he was seen dining maskless at a luxury restaurant during the state's lockdown—significantly damaged his public image. The hypocrisy of the incident, in which Newsom violated his own restrictions while urging Californians to stay home, was widely covered in the media, leading to an erosion of trust, particularly among moderate voters. This scandal, along with ongoing frustration over the state's slow economic recovery, rising homelessness, and housing costs, contributed to a sharp drop in his approval ratings, culminating in the 2021 recall election. Newsom survived the recall, but the election underscored the deep divisions in the state and highlighted his vulnerability as a leader.

Nationally, Newsom has been viewed through the lens of California's progressive image, which is often seen as either a model for the future or a cautionary tale. Outside of California, his popularity has been more variable, largely depending on how the broader country views California's progressive policies. He is widely seen as a champion of the left, with his stance on issues like climate change, healthcare, and social justice drawing significant support from progressives across the nation. However, conservatives often view him as emblematic of what they consider the worst aspects of progressive governance—high taxes, overregulation, and a focus on social policies at the expense of economic growth and practical governance. The media portrayal of Newsom has often mirrored these national divisions, painting him as either a charismatic visionary or a politician overly focused on divisive, liberal causes.

Despite his popularity among certain segments of the electorate, Newsom faces significant challenges in terms of public trust. His handling of the homelessness crisis, the wildfire disaster response, and housing affordability in California has been widely criticized. Critics argue that while Newsom has passed legislation aimed at addressing these issues, his efforts have often fallen short, leaving many of the state's most vulnerable residents without adequate support. His inability to resolve the housing crisis, with California still facing an estimated 3.5 million housing units deficit, has been a significant point of contention. For many voters, especially those in suburban and rural areas, the failure to deliver on these key issues has led to a perception that Newsom is out of touch with the practical concerns of everyday Californians.

Legacy and Long-Term Impact

As Newsom approaches the end of his governorship, his legacy will be shaped by both his successes and his failures. His tenure has been marked by ambitious progressive policies, many of which have made California a national leader in areas like climate change, healthcare, and social justice. His leadership on environmental issues, particularly his push for 100% renewable energy by 2045 and carbon neutrality, has positioned California as a global leader in the fight against climate change. Under his leadership, California has also continued to expand access to healthcare through Medi-Cal expansion and has pursued a single-payer healthcare model, though full implementation remains a distant goal.

However, Newsom's legacy is complicated by the controversies and challenges that have defined his time in office. Despite his progressive credentials, California has faced an ongoing homelessness crisis, with more than 180,000 people living on the streets, and a housing market that remains unaffordable for many residents. Critics argue that Newsom has failed to make meaningful progress on these issues, and his inability to address the root causes of homelessness and housing inequality will likely be a major point of contention when historians evaluate his governorship. His leadership during the COVID-19 pandemic was also a double-edged sword: While he initially earned praise for his swift action, his enforcement of lockdowns and mask mandates, combined with the French Laundry incident, left a legacy of division and frustration.

Newsom's legacy will also be defined by his approach to criminal justice reform. While his decision to place a moratorium on the death penalty and reduce sentences for certain nonviolent offenders aligned with his progressive values, these moves have made him a target for conservative critics who view them as overly lenient. His efforts to reduce the prison population and advocate for police reform in the wake of the Black Lives Matter movement are seen as significant achievements by some, but critics argue that Newsom's focus on criminal justice reform has not been accompanied by concrete efforts to address the rise in crime, particularly in urban areas. This disconnect between reform and public safety concerns could impact how Newsom is remembered as a leader.

In the long term, Newsom's legacy may be defined by his ambitious climate agenda and his efforts to tackle inequality. While California has made strides toward a more equitable future, the practical results of his policies will be judged in the context of the state's ongoing challenges with housing, crime, and affordability. His progressive legacy is certainly secure within the context of California's political culture, but it remains to be seen whether his vision will have the same resonance on a national scale.

Will He Be Ready for 2028?

As the 2028 presidential election approaches, Newsom's readiness to step onto the national stage will be shaped by both his record in California and the way he is perceived by the broader electorate. On one hand, his experience leading California—a state with the world's fifth-largest economy and a diverse, complex electorate—has provided him with the kind of political experience that could be valuable in the Oval Office. Newsom's ability to manage a state as large and diverse as California, balancing progressive policies with the realities of governing a complex, economically unequal society, could serve him well as a presidential candidate. One could argue that his experience dealing with the COVID-19 pandemic and navigating the economic and public health challenges that followed gives him credibility as a crisis manager.

However, one of Newsom's biggest challenges in a national run will be his lack of experience dealing with Republican pushback. California is a deeply blue state, where Newsom's policies have largely gone unchallenged by a Republican-dominated legislature. While this has allowed him to pass progressive legislation on healthcare, climate change, and criminal justice reform, it has also meant that Newsom has rarely had to engage in the kinds of bipartisan negotiations and compromises that are necessary at the national level. The ability to negotiate with Republicans and other moderates will be a crucial skill for any presidential candidate, especially if they are to have a chance in a general election. Newsom's record of polarizing leadership in California—where his progressive agenda has often been met with resistance from conservatives—could hinder his ability to build the broad coalitions necessary to govern a deeply divided country.

Moreover, Newsom's personal controversies, including the French Laundry scandal and his role in the recall election, will continue to be a challenge as he seeks national office. The lack of accountability shown during the pandemic, coupled with his personal missteps, could be a liability in a national race where the electorate demands not only policy proposals but also a sense of moral leadership and integrity. While his charisma and eloquence make him an attractive candidate for progressives, these controversies could undermine his ability to appeal to moderate and swing-state voters—key demographics for any presidential candidate.

Additionally, Newsom's leadership style may need to evolve if he hopes to succeed on the national stage. California's highly progressive policies, including its green energy push, high taxes, and emphasis on social justice reforms, are not necessarily representative of the concerns of voters in the Rust Belt, Sun Belt, or other swing states. Newsom's ability to adapt his message and find common ground with moderates and independents will be crucial for his chances in the general election.

Finally, Newsom's ability to handle national crises, from economic downturns to international conflicts, will play a significant role in determining his readiness for 2028. While his experience managing California's state budget and public health challenges provides a foundation for national leadership, the scope and complexity of national issues, particularly in foreign policy and defense, will require a broader skill set that Newsom has yet to fully demonstrate.

Gavin Newsom's potential candidacy in 2028 presents both opportunities and significant challenges. His leadership in California, while marked by progressive achievements, has also been overshadowed by controversies, personal scandals, and an inability to address some of the state's most pressing issues. His appeal to the Democratic base is undeniable, but his lack of experience in working across the aisle, coupled with his polarizing leadership style, could make it difficult for him to win over moderates and independents in a national race. As Newsom prepares for a potential 2028 presidential bid, his ability to address these challenges, adapt his policies for a national audience, and overcome his personal and political controversies will be crucial in determining his readiness to lead the nation.

Chapter 6

The 2028 Question

Final Assessment of Newsom's Leadership

Gavin Newsom is undoubtedly a skilled and charismatic politician, able to navigate the complex landscape of California's progressive politics with remarkable ease. His ability to connect with audiences, communicate his policies, and push forward a bold, progressive agenda has earned him widespread recognition within the Democratic Party. His eloquence and confidence on the national stage are undeniable; Newsom is polished, well-spoken, and capable of framing issues in a way that resonates with many Americans, particularly those on the left. His appeal to progressive voters is rooted in his support for policies like universal healthcare, climate change action, and transgender rights, which position him as a champion for marginalized communities.

However, as with all politicians, it is essential to look beyond the smooth rhetoric and polished facade that Newsom presents. Beneath his persona as a compassionate leader is a record that raises serious questions about his approach to governance. While Newsom's policies may sound appealing to many, particularly those who share his progressive values, they have had real-world consequences in California that cannot be ignored. His handling of issues such as crime, homelessness, and housing affordability has led to tangible problems within the state, ones that continue to affect the lives of millions of Californians.

In many ways, Newsom's leadership style reflects his deep understanding of political strategy: he is adept at positioning himself as a champion for social justice while pushing policies that can have a lasting, and at times, detrimental impact on the broader population. He is a master at framing arguments and making his ideas palatable to voters, but the substance of those policies—from his approach to gender-affirming care for minors to his support for transgender athletes in women's sports—has led to division, safety concerns, and social unrest. In California, the policies Newsom has championed have reshaped the state in ways that often prioritize ideological progress over practical solutions.

As a result, voters need to look past Newsom's political charm and focus on the implications of his policy record. While he may be able to win hearts and minds with his compelling rhetoric and forward-thinking promises, the reality of his leadership in California offers a cautionary tale. His approach to governance may sound appealing in theory, but the outcomes often reveal a more complex and problematic reality, one that could have lasting effects if his policies were implemented on a national scale.

The 2028 Election and Beyond

Looking toward the 2028 presidential race, Newsom's candidacy presents both an opportunity and a risk. On one hand, his ability to mobilize a large base of progressive voters and his strong national presence make him a formidable candidate. His background as the governor of California, the nation's most populous and influential state, provides him with a substantial platform to appeal to liberal voters across the country. Newsom is well-positioned to galvanize those who seek bold action on climate change, healthcare reform, and LGBTQ+ rights. His leadership on issues like gender-affirming care and transgender rights may further solidify his standing with progressive activists, positioning him as a leader who prioritizes inclusivity and social justice.

On the other hand, Newsom's record as California's governor raises serious concerns about his ability to broaden his appeal to moderates and conservatives. His handling of issues such as crime, housing, and wildfire management has drawn sharp criticism, and many of the policies he's pushed through in California have been contentious, to say the least. California, under Newsom's leadership, has faced rising costs of living, skyrocketing housing prices, and escalating homelessness, issues that continue to worsen despite Newsom's claims of progress. As Newsom seeks to extend his vision for California to the nation, he must contend with the reality that his policies, while popular in the state's liberal circles, may not resonate with voters in more conservative or swing states.

Furthermore, Newsom's tendency to eschew compromise in favor of pushing through partisan, progressive policies could become a liability on the national stage. The presidency requires the ability to unite a deeply divided nation, and Newsom's leadership style, which has often prioritized advancing progressive agendas over building bipartisan consensus, may hinder his ability to work across the aisle. His lack of experience with significant Republican opposition—a critical aspect of national politics—raises concerns about his ability to effectively govern if elected president. While California's progressive dominance has allowed Newsom to avoid these challenges to some extent, the national stage is far more complicated, and it remains to be seen whether Newsom has the political flexibility to navigate the deep divisions in Congress and among the electorate.

Public Perception and National Appeal

When it comes to public perception, Newsom is undoubtedly a polarizing figure. While he enjoys strong support among liberals, particularly those on the coasts and in urban areas, he faces significant opposition from conservatives and moderates who view his policies as extreme or harmful. His stances on issues like gender identity, climate change, and social justice reform are deeply divisive, and his leadership on these issues has often intensified the culture wars rather than providing an opportunity for meaningful dialogue and compromise.

In California, Newsom's approval ratings have fluctuated, with periods of high praise for his handling of the COVID-19 crisis, but also sharp drops in support as the state's housing crisis deepens, crime rates rise, and homelessness continues to grow. Nationally, these issues may become even more pronounced, as voters in swing states may not view Newsom's progressive policies as a solution to their local concerns. For Newsom to succeed in 2028, he would need to convince voters that his California-style solutions could work on a national scale, without alienating key constituencies.

His charisma and eloquence will likely be assets in a presidential campaign, but they must be backed by a record of pragmatic governance and effective leadership. Whether he can pivot from his progressive base in California to appeal to a broader, more diverse electorate remains uncertain.

The Implications of a Newsom Presidency

If Newsom were to become president in 2028, his policies would likely mirror much of the progressive agenda he's pushed in California. This could include further expansion of gender-affirming healthcare, the Green New Deal, and a focus on social justice reforms, particularly around criminal justice and LGBTQ+ rights. While these policies may find favor among his base, their potential to divide the country further is high. His push for sweeping social reforms without sufficient bipartisan support could intensify political polarization rather than fostering the national unity needed to address pressing issues like the economy, national security, and healthcare.

California has served as a proving ground for many of Newsom's ideas, but the broader application of these policies could come with unintended consequences. For example, while California's transition to renewable energy and its progressive stance on climate change are popular with environmental activists, they have led to rising energy costs and growing concerns about the state's energy grid. Newsom's national platform would likely include similar proposals, which could face significant resistance in parts of the country where such policies are seen as economically damaging or impractical.

Furthermore, Newsom's record on issues like crime and homelessness may hinder his ability to bring meaningful change to the nation. Despite spending billions on homelessness initiatives, California continues to face a growing crisis, and the rise in crime in cities like Los Angeles and San Francisco under Newsom's leadership has further damaged his reputation among moderates and independents.

Final Judgment: Is Newsom Ready for 2028?

Ultimately, Gavin Newsom's readiness for a 2028 presidential run is complex and multifaceted. On one hand, he is a skilled politician with the charisma, ambition, and progressive vision that could appeal to a large segment of the American electorate. On the other hand, his policies, particularly those surrounding gender identity, housing, crime, and economic equality, have led to significant challenges in California, and there is no guarantee that these approaches will translate successfully to a national stage.

Newsom's ability to unify the country—especially given the ideological divides currently shaping American politics—will be his greatest challenge. While he may be able to galvanize liberal and progressive voters, convincing moderates and conservatives that his vision for the future is the right one for America will be an uphill battle.

In the end, Newsom's political career will be judged not by his ability to charm voters, but by the tangible impact of his policies. His progressive agenda may serve him well in a primary, but in a general election, the American electorate will have to decide whether the policies that have defined his leadership in California are the right ones for the country at large.

A Note from the Author

Thank you for taking the time to read and engage with this work. In today's world, it is more important than ever to approach political decisions with a discerning eye and a critical mind. As you've read, we've explored the policies and leadership of Gavin Newsom, as well as the implications of his approach to governance. While Newsom's charisma and eloquence may captivate many, it's essential to dig deeper and consider how his policies have impacted California—and what those policies could mean for the future of the nation.

I encourage you, as a reader, to always make your own informed decisions when it comes to political leaders. Policies—not personalities—are what shape our society, economy, and the future of our country. While a candidate's likability and rhetoric can influence our opinions, it's their actions and policies that will ultimately determine the direction in which they lead. As we look toward the future, let us always remember to prioritize substance over style and critically evaluate the consequences of the policies put forth by those who seek to lead us.

Thank you again for your time and consideration. Let us continue to question, discuss, and engage in meaningful dialogue about the policies that will impact us all.

Sincerely,

Connor Strickland

Works Cited

- "California Interscholastic Federation and Transgender Athlete Policy." *CIF California*, 2021, www.cifstate.org.
- "California's Carbon Neutrality Mandate by 2045." *California Governor's Office*, 2019, www.gov.ca.gov.
- "California's Decline in Homeownership." *The New York Times*, 2021, www.nytimes.com.
- "California's Homelessness Crisis: A Closer Look at Newsom's Policies." *Los Angeles Times*, 2020, www.latimes.com.
- "California's Housing Crisis and the Strain on Its Residents." *The Sacramento Bee*, 2021, www.sacbee.com.
- "California's Medi-Cal Program and Gender-Affirming Care." *California Department of Health Care Services*, 2021, www.dhcs.ca.gov.
- "California's Outflow of Residents: The Great Migration." *California Policy Center*, 2021, www.californiapolicycenter.org.
- "California's Rising Crime Rate: What's Going Wrong?" *Fox News*, 2021, www.foxnews.com.
- "Gavin Newsom and the Future of California." *NBC News*, 2021, www.nbcnews.com.
- "Newsom's Homelessness Plan: Failures and Controversies." *San Francisco Chronicle*, 2020, www.sfchronicle.com.
- "Tesla Excluded from California EV Tax Credit Bill." *The Verge*, 2021, www.theverge.com.
- "Tesla's Role in California's Electric Vehicle Market." *Reuters*, 2021, www.reuters.com.
- "The Cost of California's Electric Vehicle Mandates." *The Los Angeles Times*, 2021, www.latimes.com.
- "The Rising Cost of Living in California." *U.S. Census Bureau*, 2021, www.census.gov.
- "California's Taxation System and Its Impact on Middle-Class Families." *The Wall Street Journal*, 2021, www.wsj.com.
- "California's Employment Development Department and the Fraud Scandal." *The Guardian*, 2021, www.theguardian.com.
- "California's Homeless Crisis: A Policy in Crisis." *National Public Radio (NPR)*, 2021, www.npr.org.

- "California's Wildfires: The Fight for Control." *The Atlantic*, 2020, www.theatlantic.com.
- "How Newsom's Policies Have Affected California's Economy." *Bloomberg News*, 2021, www.bloomberg.com.
- "Tesla: The Electric Car Giant's California Impact." *Los Angeles Times*, 2021, www.latimes.com.
- "The 2028 Presidential Race: Key Players to Watch." *Politico*, 2021, www.politico.com.
- "Gavin Newsom's Approval Ratings: What Californians Think of His Leadership." *Pew Research Center*, 2021, www.pewresearch.org.
- "California's Green New Deal and the State's Future." *The Washington Post*, 2020, www.washingtonpost.com.
- "The Electric Vehicle Market: California's Push Toward Green Energy." *New York Times*, 2021, www.nytimes.com.
- "California's Housing and Rent Crisis: The Growing Divide." *The Guardian*, 2021, www.theguardian.com.
- "The Political Rise of Gavin Newsom." *The New Yorker*, 2021, www.newyorker.com.
- "California's Homeless Crisis: Can Newsom Solve It?" *CNN*, 2020, www.cnn.com.
- "The Cost of Newsom's Climate Mandates: Analysis." *Los Angeles Business Journal*, 2021, www.labusinessjournal.com.
- "The Debate Over California's Ban on Gas Cars." *National Review*, 2021, www.nationalreview.com.
- "Gavin Newsom and the Legacy of Progressive Politics." *Time*, 2021, www.time.com.